MIKE TARGET

Also by John Mercer:

Physiotherapy as a Profession, Physiotherapy Journal 1980.

Health Care and Remedial Professionalisation, Health Manpower Review 1980.

Assessment in Paramedical Education, Assessment in Higher Education 1976.

The Story of Sidcup, Bexley Libraries and Museum Service 1989. Several articles in Primary Teaching Studies. Polytechnic of North London Journal.

MIKE TARGET

John Mercer

The Book Guild Ltd.
Sussex, England

THIS BOOK IS DEDICATED TO MY LATE BROTHER-IN-LAW.
GEORGE NEWSON
WHO DIED BEFORE THIS BOOK COULD BE WRITTEN

The Book Guild Ltd.
25 High Street
Lewes, Sussex.

First published 1990

Set in Baskerville
Typesetting by Hawks Phototypesetters Ltd.,
Copthorne, West Sussex.

Printed in Great Britain by
Antony Rowe Ltd.,
Chippenham, Wiltshire.

British Library Cataloguing In Publication Data
Mercer, John, 1923-
Mike Target
1. World War — Biographies
I. Title
940.548141

ISBN 0 86332 504 1

CONTENTS

I

D-Day

June 6th 1944 began as any other day for the men of 274 Battery, 185 Field Regiment Royal Artillery, stationed in Sheringham, Norfolk.

Dawn rose with a watery sun and a chill off the sea. The guards on the beach stood down and went back to their billets stiff and cold, for even in mid-summer the Norfolk coast can be very cool. The men came out on to the roads from their billets in empty guest houses and hotels to answer the daily roll call.

'Parade, parade, atten-shun! Answer your name — Adams,'

'Sir'

'Baker'

'Sir'

'Barnet'

'Sir,' and so on along the rows of sleepy soldiers.

Jock Sims was always the first on parade. It was a point of honour with him to get out first and be right marker. He was always smart with well polished boots and smartly hung trousers over his immaculately blancoed gaiters. George and I used to take the micky out of him. So keen, so obedient a young Scottish gunner. We preferred to make our way to parade slowly and take a pride in being last. Never late mind, but never, never first.

Parade over and our morning tasks given out to us, we went in to breakfast, our mess tins at the ready. Another Scot, whose name I cannot remember, was our battery cook. He had a good tenor voice and often in the evenings when some of us gathered together in the billet to while away the time with talk or cards, he would be called upon to sing "Ave Maria" which he did solemnly and with great purity of tone. There he was that morning dishing out scrambled dried egg and bacon with fried bread and hot sweet tea.

As we were consuming our meal the orderly sergeant came in with a clatter.

'Everyone out on parade again. At once. You can bring your tea with you.'

Surprised and not a little apprehensive we all clattered out.

'Yes, you too cookie. You come as well.'

Captain Thompson, troop commander of A troop, our troop, surveyed us for a few moments. For once Jock was not the first out.

'We have to move off at 4 pm today. I can't tell you where we are going or what is happening, but we have to be out of here and on the road by 4 o'clock. We've practised this haven't we? All the vehicles are ready. Nothing to the locals. They will know that something is happening, but our orders are to say nothing. Any questions?'

'Is this the big show, sir? Is it D-Day?'

'You'll hear more about it later. For now be ready to move at 4 pm.'

The regiment had been preparing for a landing on the French coast for several months. Because of the vast nature of the enterprise involving thousands of men and masses of military equipment, the Allied Governments had made no secret that an invasion would take place sometime in 1944. British, American, Canadian, Polish and Free French troops were camped all over Southern and Eastern England. They had been practising their various roles in conjunction with the Navy and Air Force for over a year. What was secret was the destination of the invasion force. Was it to land in the Calais area or around Dieppe or somewhere in Normandy Bay? Or even in Norway? The intention was to keep the enemy guessing until the last moment and in the event this ruse succeeded more than the commanders had dared to hope.

In preparation for D-day our trucks and armoured vehicles had been loaded with all the equipment to be carried across the Channel and then weighed on the public weighbridge at Sheringham railway station to ascertain their exact loading weight. This was to enable the landing craft and ships to be expertly packed. The engines and exhausts of the vehicles had been packed with a special water resistant compound so that each vehicle could be driven in shallow water without failing. The most vulnerable part was the exhaust, but so long as the driver maintained the engine running at a high state of revolutions and did not try to change gear, thereby reducing the flow of exhaust gases and thus allow water to enter the engine by way of the exhaust pipe, a vehicle would drive off the landing craft, down the ramp and into shallow water and then up the beach.

We spent the day at last minute preparations. Our personal gear was loaded on to the vehicles. Being a signaller I was able to tune in on the radio mounted in the gun position truck, known by the letters GBA, and hear some of the BBC news about the D-day landings which had already taken place by the initial assault troops. It was all very exciting but at the same time fear was not far away. It would be our turn next. What would be our fate on a hostile shore? How many of our lads would never return?

By 4 o'clock we were ready to move off. The Major led his battery standing in the cupola of his half-track looking back down the road as his command fell in behind him. All the vehicles had a large white star encircled by a white surround painted on the bonnet or roof. This was to show that they were part of the Allied Invasion Force, so that they would not be shot up or bombed by their own aircraft. Behind Major Draper rode two despatch riders. One was the Battery Sergeant Major and the other a Don-R to carry messages. Behind then came the Bren carrier of "A" Troop. this was an open-topped caterpillar driven vehicle with light side armour used to convey the troop commander and his forward observation staff of driver/observation post assistant, radio operator and line signaller. Because the regiment was in an infantry division, the 49th West Riding Division with a Polar Bear as the divisional emblem, the vehicles used were similar to those used by the infantry. So that when the Bren carrier of the artillery forward observation post was in the front line to support the infantry it would not be different from other infantry vehicles and therefore it would not attract enemy attention more that any other carrier. For the same reason the artillery OP in an armoured division would be located in a tank.

Following the carrier as it creaked and rattled along was George Able Baker, the command post officer's Bedford 15cwt truck carrying the gun position officer, his assistant and two signallers. I was the radio operator and co-driver. Lance-bombardier Dennis Bould was driver and co-radio operator. He was a tailor's cutter from Leeds and one of my closest friends. My other close friend was George Newson, the gun artificer, who followed in his jeep so proudly. Until very recently he had ridden a motor cycle and was delighted with his own jeep because it was safer, had better protection from the weather and carried all his tools. He was known as "Tiffy" Newson and was to be in constant demand once the guns were in action.

'Tiffy!' would go the cry, 'Tiffy — the breech is blocked' or 'Tiffy, the recoil oil is leaking out' or 'Tiffy, where's Tiffy, the firing pin is broken.'

With George rode the Troop Sergeant Major an older man and a long serving Territorial from the West Riding.

Next in column came the wire-laying truck with coils of signalling wire at the ready to be paid out when needed between command post and the forward OP. While the main means of communication was by radio, the field telephone was used as a back up and in time of static warfare a more reliable means of keeping contact. Then came the four guns of "A" troop, 25 pounders, each hauled by a "quad", a four wheel drive truck with accommodation for the gun crew of six. The truck hauled a limber holding the ammunition and the limber was hooked on to the gun. Finally came the radio truck of the troop leader (TLA). He was the third and most junior officer in the troop carrying another gun position assistant and another signaller.

There followed in similar order, five more troops, two troops to a battery making up the regiment of twenty-four gun howitzers.

In the rear position came the ammunition wagons, the supply wagons and the cook wagons. Every man in the artillery rode in a vehicle of some kind, each vehicle carefully designed to fulfil its appointed purpose and every man trained for his particular task in modern warfare.

That evening the regiment was on the move with all other units of the division, moving as dusk fell from North Norfolk towards the South. After several hours the column halted briefly and Dennis suggested that I took over the wheel of the Bedford to give him a spell off. I slipped into the driver's seat and tried hard to get the truck to move forward. I struggled to let the clutch out more gently than usual because of the heavy load and the water proofing but I kept stalling. The vehicle bucked as if driven for the first time by a learner driver and rather than risk a burnt out clutch I handed the wheel back the the Lance-bombardier.

'Sorry, Dennis,' I said, 'It's no good you'll have to drive it all the way.' All the way where? Only the officers knew the destination. All that night we drove averaging some 15 mph with short stops and blacked out lights. Those too young to remember night driving in blacked out Britain with sign-posts removed cannot imagine the difficulty and danger of such an experience.

Dozing in the back of the truck, I awoke as we bumped off the road on to grass. There were cries of "Over here" and "Okay-switch off the engine." We had arrived, but where were we? We piled out of our vehicles and made our way bleary-eyed to a marquee where breakfast was being served. To my astonishment I saw our own cooks dishing out the food. How had they got there before us?

It was 5 am on June 7th and we were somewhere in London, in a park. Was it Victoria Park in Hackney? Or was it West Ham Park? I never knew. My geography of the East End was more limited then than now.

We spent two days in the camp. It was fenced off securely and closely guarded by camp soldiers. This was as much to keep us in as to keep civilians and possible spies out. One of our cooks, a vociferous Cockney, did get out and was brought back by the Military Police. He ran the risk of a court-martial, but instead was given a severe ticking off by the commanding officer. His explanation that he had not seen his wife for a year carried less weight than the imminence of the landing in Europe and the need to have a good cook with the regiment.

On the second day we were led into a large tent to be addressed by Captain Thompson (he had had his briefing earlier by the Colonel). A large map of France was pinned to a blackboard. We sat on benches and awaited our briefing.

'Well chaps, this is it! You will have heard by now that successful landings have been made early on June 6th. They have landed on the Normandy beaches here and here (pointing to the map). British and Canadian to the east and Americans to the west. We are due to land on D+7, four days from now. We will go to the docks this afternoon and get on board our troop ships. When we get to France we will be taken ashore on Rhinos — large flat bottomed landing craft, like huge rafts. Our objective is to get as far forward as possible and take over from the assault troops of the 50th Division. The aim of 21st Army Group is to reach Mount Pincon — here it is on the map some twenty miles inland. That is what we are heading for. That's about it. We've trained for a long time for this and now it has come. Any questions?'

There were none. That mixture of elation and dread filled our hearts and stomachs.

That afternoon all the vehicles drove off with only the drivers on board. Because of that I missed the opportunity of meeting George's father who held an important position in the docks, being foreman lighterman for Tate and Lyle, and knowledgeable about all things on the river. So the non-drivers clambered aboard double decker London buses and occupied every seat. Some of the buses were from the provinces in strange livery and unexpected lettering such as "Leicester Corporation" and "Bournemouth Bus Company" on account of so many real London buses having been destroyed in the air raids.

I got a front seat upstairs and watched eagerly as the convoy of buses made its way from the camp to King George V Dock in North Woolwich. As they drove through the densely built up streets of Plaistow, the buses were surrounded by crowds of cheering East Enders. Flags flew in many windows, bunting was draped across bombed buildings, banners were stretched over the road bearing such messages as:

'Good luck — Tommy'
'Down with Hitler'
'Give them what they gave us'
'God save the King'
'God bless our lads'

Bottles of beer were passed through the bus windows. Women with tears running down their cheeks called out messages of good luck and 'Kill the bastards'. Children waved flags, hastily improvised paper wavers and streamers miraculously produced despite war time rationing. Sometimes the crowd was so great that the buses were brought to a halt and then cheer upon cheer rose to the skies. Eventually we reached the docks. By the time we had arrived most of the vehicles and guns had been winched aboard and we trooped up the gang planks and were shown our quarters. We were on a Liberty boat, made in quick time in the United States by mass production methods of an all-welded hull. I cannot recall the name of the vessel but it was one of the Empire line. Our berth was No 3 hold, my hammock slung next to the side just on the water line with five eights of an inch of steel between me and any possible mine or torpedo. The prospect did not appeal to me.

At dusk the ship slipped out of the huge dock and made its way down the Thames on the tide. London vanished behind us, no lights to be seen, no orange glow in the sky as now. I remember standing on the deck at dawn and finding the ship heaved to in company with several others near to the strange looking forts that used to guard the Thames Estuary. As we took breakfast and made up our hammocks there was a message over the loudhailer.

'Stand to. Every man stand to.'

Those of us not yet fully dressed hastily pulled on the rest of their clothes.

'We are keeping close into Dover. Our escorts are putting down a smoke screen to add to the mist. We may get shelled from German batteries on Cap Gris Nez and we may be attacked by enemy motor torpedo boats.'

Anything else he could think of we said to ourselves? What about a fleet of U-boats or a pocket battleship?

It was a long hour. We stood silent aware only of the thump-thump of the ship's engines. Nothing happened. Our three ships were clear, out of range of the enemy batteries and no longer considered in immediate danger.

We were stood down and had some tea. Later I went on deck and realised that we were hugging the coast. Bognor Regis appeared on the port side and soon the convoy swung south. As we passed the Isle of Wight more ships and their escorts joined us.

That night we all gathered below deck and drank hot chocolate. The officers led community singing and the telling of jokes which got more and more obscene as the night drew on. A warm comradeship filled the close atmosphere. Officers and men were at one in sailing to meet the common foe. Once in our hammocks and struggling to sleep we were roused by an almighty crash. God in Heaven, what ever was it? Could it be a bomb? No, it was not a bomb, it was nothing to do with the enemy. It was one of the officers of another battery who confused by sleep or drink or both had fallen down one of the hatches on to sleeping men beneath. Fortunately no one was seriously hurt, just a few bruises and bad temper.

During my night watch I stared out into the blackness of the Channel. A few stars twinkled intermittently through gaps in the clouds. The ship's wake glowed with phosopher-escence. In the distance a subdued light could be seen heading towards us. What could it be? I called my fellow guard over.

'Wally, what is that? What can it be?'

As the light grew nearer it revealed itself as a fully lighted hospital ship with red crosses illuminated prominently. It sailed by, a bright testimony to war, both reassuring as to the humanity of modern warfare and disturbing as to its wounding and destructive power. As it vanished towards the English coast and safety, the moon came out from behind the clouds and bathed the calm sea with melancholy beauty.

Dawn saw an amazing sight. We anchored a mile or two off the coast of Normandy at Arromanches. Ship upon ship surrounded us, each flying a barrage balloon as we did. Between ship and shore was a steady stream of smaller craft, landing craft of various kinds, picket boats and tugs. Further out to sea sleek destroyers moved to fresh moorings, cruisers patrolled and giant battleships could be seen. Occasionally one of the battleships would open fire upon a shore target. Huge orange flashes would be seen followed by the roar of shells overhead and a rumbling boom. No noise could be heard from the shore. The noise of battle was far inland. Night fell and all hell was let loose. The German Luftwaffe was too weak to attack the invasion fleet in daylight but come the dark it was another story. The ship's siren sounded to be echoed and re-echoed by many another ship. The distinctive "Whoop-whoop" of the destroyer siren could be heard drowning the sound of approaching aircraft. Then the Bofors guns fore and aft on our vessel opened up and, complemented by guns from many other ships, tracer shells curved up into the sky looking like flaming onions on a string. Somewhere above, German aircraft wove patterns in the sky and concentrated on bombing runs to attack the shipping. Hot shrapnel clattered on the deck. The noise was deafening. This happened several times in the night. Sometimes a sneak raider came over low and opened up with cannon shell and machine gun against ships in the fleet. In the morning when the raiders were gone and all was quiet we looked to see what damage had been done but could see no stricken vessels. I expect the raiders did some damage somewhere but it was never visible. There the ships rode at anchor as before and the hustle and bustle of the naval vessels continued as the day before.

During the next day or two we all sunbathed and read or played cards and smoked incessantly. We talked and grumbled and longed to get ashore and get on with the war. D+7 lengthened into D+9 and still we were anchored off shore. I had brought with me George Orwell's "Burmese Days" to read and I managed to read it all during our waiting period.

Every night the Luftwaffe returned and we suffered the din and the nagging worry that eventually a bomb would get us. Every day we sunbathed and gossiped. Tempers became frayed. When would we get ashore and fulfil our destiny? We had little news since the radio trucks were stored below and there could be no tuning into the news at home. At least we were told by our officers that we had not been needed on D+7 because the initial attack had gone well, but that the next day, D+13 would be our day of embarkation.

I lay in my hammock wondering what the morning would bring. After months of preparation we were about to land in France and meet the enemy face to face. After four years of war the tide was turning for the Allies, the Germans were on the defensive. But what a powerful and dangerous force they were. Had not the attack on Dieppe earlier been such a disaster? Were not the Germans so efficient and so ruthless? Were we likely to be decimated in battle and cast back into the sea? How many of us in 274 Battery would be alive in a month's time? Yet it was thrilling to land in France and liberate Europe, to bring Hitler to his knees and remove the Nazi jackboot from the necks of the occupied Europeans. It was a noble enterprise and it was a privilege to take part in what seemed to us to be a crusade of good against evil. With these mixed emotions occupying my mind I fell into a fitful sleep.

We were awakened at first light and began to prepare for embarkation. From the deck we could see the Rhinos rising and falling with the swell against the ship's side. We could see something else too. Far out to sea, but moving steadily nearer we could see tugs pulling floating lengths of concrete. Section upon section of sea wall was being towed into the Bay of Arromanches. This was to be the Mulberry Harbour which was blueprinted and constructed section by section in Britain and then transported to the French coast and sunk near the shore to provide an artificial harbour protected against rough Channel seas by a screen of old ships deliberately sunk off shore. Of this we had only an inkling as at that time the harbour was only just begun and our eyes were never to see the completed harbour as by the time of its completion we were into the Normandy bocage and the fierce fighting west and north of Caen.

The vehicles and guns were winched down to the bobbing Rhinos. It was quite difficult to climb hand over fist down the rope curtain from the ship's deck to the landing raft. The Rhino rose and fell against the ship's side several feet and the gap between Rhino and ship widened and narrowed with each vertical move. One got to the bottom of the rope curtain and waited, pack on back, weapon slung over shoulder, until the craft rose and simultaneously moved in against the side of the ship. Then one let go and jumped to land safely, if a little unsteadily, upon the patterned metal deck of the landing craft.

When our Rhino was fully loaded the Royal Marines in charge opened up the engines, cast off from the ship and headed slowly towards the shore. There was a gentle swell. The shore line became clearer. Then the ramps were lowered and the vehicles and the guns moved forward. Every vehicle and gun on our Rhino made the beach without mishap. The water proofing had worked despite our misgivings. The only misfortune was an individual one. One of the gun crew, a bombardier, missed his footing and fell into three feet of water. His laughter was only second to that of his companions.

Ashore in France and not a casualty! The vehicles formed up and drove off the sandy beach within the white tapes put there by the engineers to denote a route cleared of mines. From inside GBA I could see only the dunes as they receded. The radio net was being established. Earphones on head and microphone in hand I tuned in to the wavelength given to us.

'Hello Able Baker report my signals,' came from control, located within the Major's half track.

Each radio in the net tuned in the signal given and reported back in turn.

'Hello Able Baker One. Strength 3.'

'Hello Able Baker Two. Strength 2.'

'Hello Able Baker Three. Strength 4.'

And so on until all the stations in 274 Battery were "on net" and in good communication.

2

Ashore

The efficiency of a field battery can be measured in several ways: the accuracy of its fire; the speed at which the guns can be loaded, aimed and fired; and the speed at which a battery on the move can be deployed and put into action. All these measures had been rehearsed in mock and live exercises in England. Now it was to be the real thing. Somewhere ahead "A" troops's company of the Duke of Wellington's Light Infantry Regiment was moving forward. The Wellingtons were taking over from front line units of the 50th Division which had carried the initial assault. From the back of the truck all I could see was white dust thrown by the moving vehicles. Occasionally, through the white dust could be seen glimpses of buildings, a cross roads, a steep hedgerow. The convoy moved slowly bumping over uneven road surfaces and halting briefly from time to time because of traffic hold-ups.

Suddenly the order came over the radio into my head phones.

'Halt — action left!'

I repeated the order loudly, 'Halt — action left!'

Lieutenant Cannell, our gun position officer, riding in the front of the truck, directed the vehicle into a nearby field and sent his command post assistant racing off to indicate where the four guns were to be deployed. Each quad, limber and gun drove in to the field and the gunners fell out of their cabs on to the grass. Hastily the guns were unlimbered, the limber pulled to the left, the gun pulled on to its firing platform and the gun sight screwed into place. The bombardier on each gun lined up his sight on to the aiming post driven into the ground ahead and to the left of the guns.

As each gun was correctly aligned the bombardier struck his rear with his right hand and the rest of the crew knelt at their appointed positions. Although a driver/operator I had been trained, like all artillerymen, in gunnery and knew the gun drill off by heart. The gun sergeant in rear of the gun raised his arm high.

'No 1 gun ready!'

In a few seconds all the guns were ready and "A" troop waited tensely for their first experience of action.

Meantime GBA had disgorged the gun position officer's other assistant, Fred Dalton, who was joined by Lieutenant Small, the troop leader, from TLA. Together they mounted the firing table on its tripod and busied themselves with calculations using the director.

'Troop target! Map reference 678943.' The fire orders came over the radio and were repeated. From the map reference was worked out the distance from the guns to the target, the angle of sight to ensure that the shells would clear any obstruction and the compass bearing necessary to make sure that the shells would fall in the right place.

'Troop target H.E.119 charge 3! Bearing zero 106 degrees. Angle of sight 2 degrees — range 4,800. Fire by order!'

The gun sergeants reported their readiness.

'Fire!'

The four guns fired. There were four flashes and an explosion overhead.

The four guns fired again. Once more an explosion.

'Stop firing!' A desperate shout came from No 3 gun

What was happening? No order to cease fire over the radio had been received. What was happening? Were we being shelled back by the enemy even as we fired?

'Stretcher bearers!' came the cry.

The guns fell silent. Lieutenant Small ran over to Sergeant Gawler's gun. Gunner Dickenson, a youngster with a hare-lip and curly hair so quiet and inoffensive, lay badly wounded on the ground near to the gun limber. His sergeant stood ashen-faced beside him. He had forgotten in the excitement of the first engagement with the enemy, to look up the gun barrel and check that he had indeed angle of sight clearance. He had not and as a consequence the two shells fired from his gun, and his alone, had hit a tall tree only twenty yards from the gun muzzle. The shells had exploded and rained shrapnel down on to his own gun. As a consequence poor Dickenson lay wounded and the first casualty in the troop was caused by our own foolishness.

The guns were moved back nearer to the road to be away from the trees and they fired no more that day.

Night fell and the crew of GBA had to decide where to sleep. Should they dig slit trenches? The ground was very hard. Should they sit in the truck all night? Should they lie beneath the stars wrapped in blankets and groundsheets? This soldier decided to do the latter. It was strange to lie on one's back and look up at the dark velvet sky illuminated by the twinkling of innumerable stars. There was little moon that night. The front was strangely quiet. The coast was not. Anti-aircraft fire could be distantly heard and shells could be seen in the sky bursting over the landing beaches. Sometimes the crackle and boom of shell bursts were audible; sometimes the shells burst silently in the sky being so much further away. An aircraft reverberated from inland. As it passed into Allied territory anti-aircraft guns defending the forward forces opened up and the bursting of shells occurred immediately overhead. Within seconds I could hear the swish of shell fragments hitting the grass beside me. One landed on the bonnet of GBA with a clatter. I came to the conclusion that sleeping in the open under the stars was not a good idea and I rolled myself cocoon-wrapped under the modest protection of GBA making sure that my head did not lie under the engine sump.

It was my turn to man the radio after four hours (I was to man the radio two hours on four hours off for the next twelve weeks, interspersed with much longer hours when up with the infantry under fire: a system which led in the end to almost permanent exhaustion). Later that morning we got the order to move to what I believe was called Audrieu.

Our troop moved into an orchard on the left of a narrow

road. "B" troop moved into a similar orchard on the other side of the road. The guns had no sooner been layed-on to the aiming post and reported ready than fire orders came through. The GPO and his staff operated under an apple tree, the radio operator sitting on the grass beside them using an extension lead. I was off duty and so went across to Sergeant Robert's No 1 gun to lend a hand with ammunition carrying. The first target was a Mike Target, that is to say a regimental target of twenty-four guns linked through the radio net and the regimental command post. The range was under 2,000 yards. The second target was also a Mike Target, the range dropping to 1,500 yards. By this time armour piercing tank shells were whizzing almost silently through the orchard aimed at our tanks, invisible to us on the forward edge of the orchard. Troop Sergeant Major Beckwith was hit by a shell splinter and was sitting on the ground cursing loudly and nursing his leg (the extent of the injury was more than we realised and he did not return to the regiment until we were in Belgium in December). The order came '800 yards — open sights!'

Our gun crews prepared to fire their limited supplies of armour piercing shells directly at enemy tanks as soon as they appeared. Some of our infantrymen ran through the orchard looking fearfully behind them. The gun crews stood steadily behind the limited protection of their gun shields. Lieutenant Cannell and his staff still sat under the apple tree looking unhappy and very vulnerable. We all craned our eyes ahead expecting to see German tanks emerging from the far end of the orchard. The shells ceased to whizz. The rattle of small arms fire died away. Silence reigned. It seemed as if the enemy advance had been halted and that the Germans had stabilised their forward positions about 1,500 yards beyond us. News came that Jock Sims had been killed by a spent armour-piercing shell. It had sliced him in half as he was carrying a 25-pounder shell to the breach of his "B" Battery gun across the road. Poor Jock! His smartness and keenness had availed him nothing. News also came that Aston, the equipment repairer, had died. Aston used to say how safe he was back at regimental headquarters, but this was an illusion. He had jumped out of the back of the truck he was riding in with his Sten sub-machine gun over his shoulder. The loaded magazine of 38mm calibre bullets was in the gun and as his feet touched the ground the shock of the impact triggered off the gun and blew away the top of his head. Here was a lesson all had to learn. Never sling a Sten gun over your shoulder with a loaded magazine in position. Carry it in a pouch or in a hip pocket, but never, never have it on the gun until you need to fire it. The Sten was a crude little sub-machine gun made in numerous backyard workshops for about seven shillings (so the story went). Once the trigger was pulled the heavy bolt flew back inserting the new bullet and holding itself by inertia just long enough to fire the round before being thrown back once more. So if the loaded gun was tapped on the ground it would begin to fire on its own accord unless the safety catch was on. And even if it was on the vibration of any impact could dislodge it and the gun would fire uncontrollably. Poor Aston. Poor Jock. Two dead and two wounded so soon.

Later that day I wandered across to 386 Battery to see if I could find my old pal, Maurice Tyerman, another radio operator. They were further to the left and further forward. Apparently their guns had actually engaged enemy tanks when the order "open sights" had been given.

'Well Mercer J.,' said Maurice in his familiar Yorkshire accent, 'this is the real thing all right. I wish we were back in Sheringham right now, queuing up for the pictures!'

I could only agree with him.

News came back from the O.P. (Observation Post) that what had happened earlier that day had been a heavy mortar bombardment by the Germans on the newly deployed Duke of Wellington's Regiment. The company that "A" troop was attached to had been badly shaken by the accuracy and severity of the mortar fire and had suffered many casualties. When tanks and accompanying infantry of the Panzer Lehr Division moved forward behind the mortar attack many of the British infantry fled in terror. Captain Thompson and his carrier crew remained in position and brought down the fire of the Mike Targets until the attack was halted by our shell fire, our tanks and dug in anti-tank guns, and forced to withdraw to the positions held by the Wellington's.

Other infantry units had been more successful so that later that afternoon we saw lines of German prisoners shuffling along the lane. Those not on duty crowded to the side of the orchard and into the lane to see the prisoners. We had not seen German soldiers in the flesh before. We had never seen German soldiers in defeat and as prisoners. They came past us dressed in field grey. They were dirty and dishevelled. They were tired and unshaven. Some were wounded with bandaged arm or head. Their shuffling feet churned up the all-pervading white dust. All this was too much for Fred Dalton, our lantern jawed GPO assistant from Leeds. He was fair haired and light skinned. Many of the prisoners were dark-haired with swarthy complexions.

'Call yourselves the master race, the Herrenfolk!' He shouted (I can hear his voice now). 'Look at you, you bloody miserable lot of bastards. There's not an Aryan among you!'

Several days later we saw fresh infantry marching up the lane to the front.

'Look there's Smithy. Wasn't he with us when we landed? Why is he marching with the infantry?'

Some of us managed to walk beside him for a few moments and to draw out what had happened to him. He had been taken ill when landing and had been sent to field hospital near Bayeux (which, incidentally, had been preserved from any damage). Upon his quick recovery he had been sent into the infantry because of their heavy casualties. Off Smithy marched. A few moments later the commanding officer of 185 Field Regiment drove along in his jeep on a tour of inspection. Known affectionately as "Charlie Handlebars" on account of his magnificent moustache, he was informed of the situation of Gunner Smith.

'Driver,' he commanded, 'catch up with those men in front.'

The jeep accelerated away into the near distance. How far could he go before being fired on? For round the corner of the orchard the lane was under direct observation of the enemy.

A few minutes later the jeep returned bearing not only the colonel but also Gunner Smith. It passed the gun

The author in 1942 at the Signals Training Regiment in Scarborough.

position and sped to the rear. Much later we learned from Smithy what had happened.

'Charlie Handlebars came along in 'is jeep and to the sergeant-major who was escorting us said, "Halt this column!" Being 'im a colonel and the other only being a warrant officer, 'e 'ad to obey orders. So Charlie says, "This man belongs to me. 'E 's one of my best drivers and you can't 'ave 'im!" Then to me "Fall out and get up 'ere in the back of my wagon" And off we goes leaving the sergeant major speechless.'

You can imagine how delighted we all were to hear of this event and how much it raised our morale and the prestige of the colonel.

The battery remained in the orchard until the end of July. The fighting ebbed and flowed. Much of the fiercest fighting went on to our left as attack after attack was launched to capture Caen. On our own front there was daily skirmishing and some heavy exchanges. Our guns were sometimes within range to support the activities outside Caen.

But the main objective of the division was to capture the sprawling village of Tilly-sur-Seulles. A village which change hands several times and of which only the church and rectory remaind standing when all the fighting was over.

3

The gun position in the orchard

Having got over the shock of the initial enemy attack as we moved into the orchard, all ranks set out to build themselves shelters against shell, bomb and weather. There was a strong gale and heavy rain several days after our arrival (the Mulberry Harbour in the course of construction was badly damaged). George, Dennis and I decided upon a common dug-out and between times of duty on gun maintenance and manning the radio we dug a neat trench behind the gun position and covered it with branches, earth and a ground sheet. But before we could do this to our satisfaction we had to dig out a shelter for the command post. A hole some four feet deep and six feet square was dug and a canvas roof was erected kept up by branches and tied down by rope and pegs. Anyone seated would be below ground level. Any one standing up would be head and shoulders above the ground. Lieutenant Cannell felt uneasy about this vulnerability and over the next few days made us dig deeper until a six-footer would be below ground level when standing up at the firing table. Lieutenant Cannell was six feet two inches and still felt slightly vulnerable. The guns were also dug in and covered with camouflage netting. By the third day all the men of "A" troop had their dug-outs well below ground level and felt safe to sleep. Blanket rolls were undone, ground sheets were laid out and the sleep of the just experienced by one and all until fire orders began. On about the third day a big programme of fire was laid down to support an attack. Two hours before dawn the guns began a creeping barrage behind which the infantry with supporting tanks moved forward. Round after round was fired, the night sky illuminated by constant flashes of gunfire and the countryside filled with the heavy roll of the bombardment. As dawn broke the guns ceased and there was a strange silence. Acrid cordite smoke assaulted the nostrils and drifted through the orchard. It had been an Uncle Target, that is to say a divisional target embracing three regiments of 25 pounders and a regiment of 5.5 guns. The silence did not last long. Sustained mortar fire could be heard like the thumping of a table by a hundred hands, and the rattle of machine gun fire was audible in the distance. First the "rat-a-tat-tat" of the Bren gun used by our infantry then the "pop-pop-br-br-br" of the German Spandau in reply.

A paragraph on the respective machine guns will be helpful.

The Bren had a magazine holding some thirty bullets. A full magazine could be easily exchanged for an empty one. The Bren was quite light, firing single shots or automatic fire, precisely and accurately. The Spandau was fed by a belt of bullets, sometimes two simultaneously. It fired very fast but not very accurately. It sprayed bullets like a hose pipe. The aiming shots were always followed by a fast burst. The sound once heard was unmistakeable. A Spaudau unexpectedly firing close to your position was an alarming experience.

The German soldiers manning the coastline had been flung back by the massive assault on D-Day. The enemy reserves were quickly concentrated and pushed forward to try to force the invading Allies back on to the beaches. The early days were crucial to the Germans before they were to be outnumbered by successive landings of Allied troops. Reinforcements from Central and Southern France were rushed to Normandy and flung piecemeal into the battle to stem the Allied attack. Two Panzer Divisions were in our battle zone, the Panzer Lehr and the 21st Panzer, both of which had elements of SS troops in them. In the fierce fighting that summer in Normandy the Germans became gradually outnumbered and outgunned but their armour was always superior in armour protection and gun power.

Fighting in the "bocage", small fields surrounded by high banks topped with hedges, and fighting in the cider orchards, was marked by short visibility. The enemy dug their tanks into the hedgerows and hid them thoroughly, machine gun nests were cut into the high earth banks and mortar and gun crews moved from cover to cover in the orchards and villages using cellars and ditches to shelter in. Our infantry had to advance across small fields and along hedgerows in the teeth of mortar and machine gun fire. Our tanks were constantly shot up and set on fire by the deadly 88mm guns of Tiger and Panther tanks dug into invisibility. Snipers camouflaged into the background tied themselves into trees and fired upon our advancing soldiers from the rear once they were well past them. Often the sniper was undetected. Once he was spotted he was shown little mercy. On one advance not long after our arrival at Duoy St Marguerite, Captain Thompson was seriously wounded by such a sniper. He was standing up in his Bren carrier accompanying his company of infantry when a sniper fired a burst at the carrier. Bullets from the Spandau tore across the carrier piercing the officer's neck in three places. He fell in a pool of blood. Fortunately the three bullets had missed his main arteries and jugular vein. Within a short while he was whisked to the field hospital and flown back to England. We were not to see him again until September when he returned to take up command of "A" troop. The radio operator was also wounded though less seriously and these casualties led to a re-organisation of the troop. Another captain, whose name I cannot remember, was moved in to take command of "A" troop and the radio operators placed in a pool so that those previously attached to the gun position took a turn with the observation post. Accordingly in the last few days of June I was driven up to the carrier with Jim Pearce to take over from the two other signallers. But before continuing with the front line battle narrative let me tell you of some of the more domestic events that took place in our orchard near to Audrieu.

Our food was cooked and prepared in the wagon lines and driven out each day to each troop in a 3-ton lorry. On the sight of the 3-tonner swaying out of the dust filled lane and into the orchard there was a shout of "grub up".

Soldiers not on duty lined up by the tail gate and gathered rations for the day for themselves and for their mates on duty. Mess tins were held out and in each was plopped breakfast, dinner and tea. Breakfast would be porridge, or bread, margarine and jam, or sardines, or sometimes tinned bacon that had been boiled. This was in cellophane in tins and the cellophane strips used to sail across the orchard in the wind leaving behind in the air the smell of fatty boiled bacon. Dinner would be a slice of spam and army biscuit. Tea would be more hard biscuit or a slice of bread. Tea to drink would be poured into each man's mug: hot and very sweet.

It was a task of ingenuity to separate the food into the three meals. Sometimes the task was totally unsuccessful. Sardines became trapped in porridge, margarine and jam became mixed in with the spam, the bacon (complete with cellophane wrapping) congealed with the bread. We often cursed, frequently laughed at our meals — but we never starved. We had fresh food whenever possible. We also had composition rations — compo for short — which were pre-packed concentrated food. Compo tea contained tea, sugar and milk in little blocks. It tasted peculiar but was better than nothing. Compo chocolate and compo biscuits were good to eat. During an engagement, especially when with the infantry doing target spotting we had only compo rations. It was not a good idea to attempt to drive a 3-tonner close to the enemy! On the gun position we often brewed our own tea. A small hole was dug in the ground and bags of discarded cordite were burned to heat the water to make the tea. Each brass shell case contained three charges, that is to say bags of cordite, coloured red, blue and white. If the fire order was charge three all the bags were used. If the order was charge two, then the blue bags were discarded. If charge one then blue and red bags were discarded. Once discarded they could never be used again since every shell case contained three bags. So the spares were used to heat the water for tea, washing and shaving. Cordite packed into a confined space explodes, but in the open it burns brightly and fiercely with much concentrated heat. Having ready access to this source of fuel was a perquisite available only to the artillery, and to a lesser extent to the tank gunners.

At the end of our second week in the orchard the order was given that every one should take a bath. We had not bathed since leaving Sheringham. When my turn came I was led by one of the bombardiers with five others to a farm house a few hundred yards back from our position. In an outbuilding was a large metal vat used for cider making. This was half filled with warm water and we drew lots to establish order of entrance. I seem to recall that I was second to last so that by the time I had stripped off and clambered in the water was brown with soap and dirt and scum. Nevertheless it was good to wash all over and to stimulate the circulation with some vigourous towelling. I occasioned some amusement and ribbing because beneath my battledress trousers instead of army issue underpants I wore a pair of cotton pyjamas! This practice I had learned earlier in my army life as woollen battledress irritated my legs and I was fearful of getting some rash when living rough. Our washing over, the bombardier produced a bottle from behind his back and bade us have a tipple. It was Calvados, the potent Normandy brandy distilled from cider. It was immediately renamed Firewater. Back at the gun position there was a frenzy of clothes washing and the trees were soon festooned with grey looking underwear and rinsed through socks. One day we heard that a despatch rider belonging to our battery was missing. It was Purvis, the Major's Don-R. We could not think what had happened to him. He had driven up to the forward positions once or twice behind the Major's half-track but there had been no report of any accident. Later we heard that he had been picked up by the military police on the beaches and had been placed under arrest and charged with desertion. It seemed that riding behind the half-track, semi-blinded with dust and not able to hear anything save the rattle and screech of the vehicle, he had become terrified of being killed by an unseen burst of machine gun fire or unexpected shell burst. His terror had become so strong that he had driven his motorcycle as far as he could from danger, abandoned it and sought refuge in a ruined house. He had never been a popular fellow in the battery. He sneered at others and boasted about himself so much that he had few if any friends. The general feeling amongst us was contempt

The Three Stooges — taken 20th December 1944
Left, John Mercer. Centre, Dennis Bould, Right, George Newson

for his cowardice. We wondered what the outcome of his court martial would be. We never found out exactly what did become of him but we were led to believe that he was sent back to England to be treated for battle fatigue. In the First World War he would have been shot. We felt glad that we were fighting in the Second World War.

4

With the infantry

It is only now forty years on and having read several books of military history (notably Macdonald Hastings "OVERLORD") that I realise the heavy casualties suffered by our infantry and our armour. Our brigade was down to half strength after three weeks in battle. Other units were brought in to make up the numbers and they in turn were more than decimated. Of this I was ignorant at the time. One man's war up at the front is limited to the nearest hedgerow, the next ditch, the furthest trees that can be seen. Unless one is an officer of staff rank the stage of war is very limited. The Germans lost heavily, too, and in the final stages of the Normandy campaign excessively. But in the first two months of the fighting, man for man we lost more. Despite overwhelming air and artillery superiority the fighting in those summer months was far tougher than the Allies had expected. I recall Major Draper remarking to a fellow officer.

'The fighting here in the bocage is much worse than in the Western Desert.'

Being a gunner, I was in a safer position than the infantry or the tank crews or the assault engineers. But this was not so when I took my turn at the forward observation post and operated with the infantry. When the jeep took Jim Pearce and myself up to the Bren carrier to relieve the existing crew that was already in the forward area we stopped by a steep bank.

'This is as far as we can go,' said the driver. 'I'll walk

with you to the O.P. Watch out for snipers. It's all quiet now, but for God's sake keep your eyes open.'

We followed a narrow farm track between towering hedgerows and then made our way across a small enclosed field. I felt menaced on all sides. There was a deathly silence. The sweet and sickly smell of dead cows came on the air. My scalp prickled with fear. Was there a sniper in one of those trees? We climbed through the bank where a tank had forced an entrance and down another farm track. Halfway down was the carrier. We were greeted by its occupants.

'Be very quiet. Jerry is only a couple of hundred yards away. It's all quiet now,' said the captain, 'But last night there was an attack here and we have a souvenir to prove it.' Sticking out of the exhaust grille on top of the carrier was a mortar bomb, its fins clearly showing.

'I don't like to move it or the carrier, lest it goes off.'

We all stared at it. The fins stared back. One of the infantrymen walked up, sub-machine gun at the ready.

'You'll have to get the bomb squad up to take it out,' he said.

The OP assistant stared at it then said, 'All of you stand back, I'm going to pull it out.'

We all stood back respectfully as the bombardier climbed into the side compartment and examined the bomb and its situation. Then very carefully he pulled the bomb out of the exhaust casing ensuring that the long fuze on its nose did not make contact with anything. He passed it to the infantryman who laid it reverently down on its side in the grass.

'Well done,' we all whispered, 'Well done. You've got a lot of nerve.'

The crews having changed, I was given the task of fetching new batteries for the No 19 set. This entailed going back the way we had come and picking two heavy batteries (called "dags") from the jeep. It was not too bad carrying the old batteries from the carrier as I had some help. But once back at the jeep, it drove off leaving me two "dags" to manage on my own. I picked up one of the brutes and staggered back to the carrier. It was a fiercely hot day and I sweated profusely under my load. My sweat was multiplied by my anxiety in crossing the enclosed field with its possibility of snipers or a fresh mortar attack. I reached the carrier, connected up the "dag" and returned for the second. Again I sweated and struggled with the second "dag" with all its attendant anxieties. But fortunately nothing happened — all was still.

The infantry commander wanted to send a patrol forward to see just how far the enemy were away as contact had been lost with them during the night's bombardment. A No 18 set was hoisted on my back and I was sent with the patrol along the pathway towards the side of a steep bank. The modern "walkie-talkie" had not yet been invented and the set I was using was the lightest that could be used in the field. It had quite a short range, in this case back to the carrier, and was awkward to carry and to use. The patrol reached the bank and stopped. A section was sent further forward, cautiously crawling and running.

There was no response from the enemy. They had either withdrawn much further or they were lying low not wanting to give their positions away. The section came back to the platoon officer and reported seeing Germans dug in some 100 yards ahead.

'We looked at them and they looked at us,' reported the section leader, laconically.

The infantry and artillery officers conferred for a few moments.

'Let's not stir up a hornet's nest,' agreed the two.

As a consequence the artillery observation post was moved back to the carrier, and possible targets were registered on the map for future reference.

I cannot recall how long I stayed with that carrier. It might have been one tense but uneventful day or it might have been longer. In any event I was moved back to the Major's half-track at battalion headquarters to act as second radio operator there. The battalion headquarters of the Wellington's was established in and around a ruined farmhouse that had changed hands several times in the fighting. The lull that had held for several days still continued and when off radio watch for a couple of hours, I wandered over to the far edge of the farm buildings where orchards fell away to the right and found to my delight

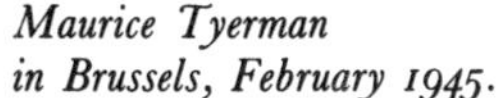

Maurice Tyerman in Brussels, February 1945.

Maurice from 386 Battery who, like me, had been sent up from the guns to act as an O.P. operator.

'It's nice and quiet round here,' I opined to Maurice.

He laughed. 'You may think so but there are lots of Germans not far away in the orchard.'

'No, you must be mistaken, we are some way back from the nearest enemy. Look I've got a map here to prove it,' I insisted. Maurice shook his head and laughed again.

'You never could read maps, Mercer,' and concentrated on his compo tea. I was nettled by this and was sure Maurice was wrong. Little did I know how right he was, and little did I know how many times in future years he was to tell this tale against me with many a gleeful chortle.

As dusk fell Maurice and his crew rattled off. I returned on foot to the half track and took over the radio on listening watch. With earphones clamped to my head I spent four hours of listening; an occasional request to "repeat my signals", some harmonics bringing distant and obscure messages, and a soft but perpetual hiss of radio static. In the middle of the night I was relieved by the signal bombardier and bedded down in a fox-hole dug and previously occupied by some enemy infantryman. He had left behind his tattered waterproof cape (far inferior in quality to that issued to me) which proved very useful as it commenced to rain quite heavily. Although it was June 30, it was not a warm night and without my blankets I was grateful for the thin cover of the cape. I slept fitfully, half standing, half lying. Just before dawn a fierce and sustained bombardment opened up all along our front. Hundreds of heavy mortar shells crashed and reverberated in the fields and orchards around us. The eerie sound of the Nebelwerfer was repeatedly heard. This multiple mortar fired bombs by rocket in quick succession with a whooping noise that was both unpleasant and unforgetable. I crouched down in my little hole. Maurice had been right about the German proximity. It was now July 1, 1944 and my twenty-first birthday. Instead of being the centre of a warm family party in England I was in the centre of a pitched battle. Instead of being given celebratory presents from relatives and friends I was being showered with earth from exploding mortar bombs.

The bombardment lasted some ten minutes. It was followed by an enemy assault of great strength led by tanks and infantry. Under the fire, orders directed from the halftrack some ten feet to my right, sent our shells whining overhead to fall with a crash on targets invisible to me. Mike Target after Mike Target was called. I was aware of stray shells falling short and exploding behind me. On the left some Sherman tanks were moving up to re-inforce our troops. One was struck by an armour piercing shell fired from an 88mm. gun. It "brewed up" and its crew jumped out in haste as it caught fire and exploded. One man was in flames. Machine gun bullets arrived, mostly spent and falling on the ground with a swish and tinkle. But as the epicentre of the battle got nearer the bullets swished all around dangerously. A thick pall of smoke hung over the orchards and clung to the ruined farmbuildings. "A" Troop carrier came out of the smoke and swung round in the lee of the halftrack. The crew that had relieved me so recently were smoke blackened. Our infantry were falling back and occupying the fox holes around battalion H.Q. The Shermans were halted and firing at advancing German tanks obscured from my view. The din was deafening.

A sergeant half ran, half crawled from the edge of the house to the command post.

'The Germans are across the corner of the yard and have the field of fire in front of us — the wires are cut.'

He doubled back again keeping low. The firing in front had become less intense.

Major Draper called out to me, 'Gunner, will you see if you can mend the wire:'

Although radio was the main means of our communication, signallers also ran out telephone lines from the guns to the observation post connecting a "Don 5" handset (battery operated) at each end. The wire forward to "B" Troop OP had been severed. I stood up and crawled out of my hole. Should I take my Sten with me? I would not have free hands if I did, and after the lesson of Aston I was not going to sling it over my shoulder. So I left it on top of the fox hole and, wiring knife and pliers at the ready, dodged forward to find the wire. There it was, a muddy yellow cable. I followed it along the ground gingerly, fully expecting a fatal burst of machine gun fire.

No fire came. I reached the end of the wire and laid down to see where the other broken end might be. I crawled forward a little way and could see no trace of it. I made my way back to the half track and called to the Major that the wire was too badly destroyed to mend. He accepted my report and I thankfully resumed my hole. As I did so there was a renewed exchange of small arms fire from the right.

Out of the orchard ran three German soldiers in S.S. uniform. They were bare headed. They ran for their lives looking fearfully behind them. Their faces were white and convulsed with terror. One of them was in tears. They threw away their guns and ran on, hands held high in the air.

'Nicht schliessen!! Nicht schliessen!'

They were ignored by our soldiers and they ran on to our

rear to vanish into the next plantation. Presumably they were taken prisoner by others. Very few combat soldiers want to be bothered with prisoners, as I was later to find out for myself, for they have an objective to reach and any of their number removed to take charge of prisoners weakens their strength and resolve.

Then a second mortar bombardment followed accompanied by the roar of tanks moving forward. It was impossible to tell if it were the enemy or our own tanks advancing. Our guns opened up once more on further targets. In the din I became aware that the Shermans on the left had moved forward. But three remained silent and impotent.

In the lull that followed it became my turn to man the radio. News filtered back about "B" Battery OP. The carrier had been positioned under the lee of a farm wall and during the dawn attack a Tiger tank had lumbered out of the bocage and opened fire upon it. The carrier had reversed through a gateway and taken refuge on the other side of the wall. Whereupon the giant enemy tank had smashed through the wall, appeared on the other side and advanced once more on the carrier. The crew jumped our and ran for their lives pursued by a hail of bullets. The troop commander hid from the tank as it tracked along the wall and then found to his horror that it was coming through the wall again. He fled to the shelter of a farm building amidst a rain of bullets and the discharge of a high explosive shell from the tank's 88mm. The Tiger halted and began to demolish the building with more high explosive rounds. Captain Hawkins managed to dodge out of the other side of the building and took cover with his crew and men of the Wellington's. The luckless troop commander, when the battle was over, was taken to hospital in a state of total shock and never returned to the regiment.

As night fell the fires from the burning buildings and smouldering vehicles glowed ahead. The occasional flash of an exploding mortar bomb lit up the darkness. The "pop-pop-brurp" of a Spandau was heard from time to time. I was back in my old foxhole linked by telephone line to the guns. The radio was turned off since the batteries were run down and no new ones had been brought up. I would be needed to pass any fire orders during the night. The British position at Rauray had been held despite the fierceness of the enemy attack and they were not expected to launch another for a while.

It began to rain once more and with the German cape around me I huddled in my refuge listening to any bleep that might come on the telephone and considering what a 21st birthday I had spent.

The next thing I knew was being shaken.

'Wake up, soldier, wake up. We thought you were dead!'

I struggled to make out where I was and what was going on. It was our signals' sergeant and his two linemen.

'We've been buzzing you all night. At first we thought the wire must have been cut but as we got near to you we thought you must be dead. But you've been bloody asleep. What the bleeding hell do you mean by it, dragging us out half through the night on a fool's errand? Do you know we haven't had a wink of sleep ourselves for twenty-four hours!'

I mumbled that I was sorry. That I had not intended to go to sleep. I, too, had not had sleep for an even longer length of time. The signal sergeant cursed me roughly for a few moments and led his crew away. Would I be reported for dereliction of duty? Would I be shot? I would have been in World War 1. But I was not reported and that was my first of three escapes from possible military court martial that I encountered. I am eternally grateful to that sergeant who I later discovered was suffering from severe piles and was in fact sent back home for an operation not long after.

In the morning things were still quiet though there was the odd burst of fire and rumble of guns in the distance. Charlie Handlebars drove out in his jeep to meet his forward crews and to review the situation. Lieutenant Youlton was standing beside his carrier talking to his new crew when a stray shell burst nearby showering splinters. I was standing near to the halftrack some twenty feet away and saw that he had been hit. I was the first to realise what had happened and dashed forward pulling out my first aid dressing as I ran. His nose had been neatly removed by a flying splinter leaving a small, piece of bone just below his eyes. He knew he had been wounded because of the blood pouring down his face and on to his tunic, but he could not see or feel just how he had been wounded. I carefully placed the field dressing over the wound and fastened the bandages firmly round the back of his head.

'Are you all right, Peter?' called the Colonel from his jeep.

'Yes, I think so, sir,' replied the bewildered young officer.

The colonel drove up to the carrier and taking Peter by the arm sat him down in the jeep.

'You'll be all right,' he said, 'just a little wound, I'll drive you to the regimental aid post.'

'Thank you sir,' said Lieutenant Youlton, very pale and still uncertain as to the nature and extent of his wound.

The colonel gave me a quick nod and a hard look and drove away at speed. That afternoon our relief crews arrived and we were taken back to the gun position some two miles to the rear.

Thus ended the battle for Rauray where there is now to be found a war memorial to the men of the 49th Infantry Division who fell in those orchards and enclosed fields in the summer of 1944, fighting against the Panzer Lehr and the 9th S.S. Panzer Divisions.

The guns still remained in the orchards near to Audrieu for some little time. I did my turn and turn about at gun position and OP, sitting in the command post when on the radio or sleeping in the dug out shared with Dennis and George. When at the former I had to remain alert to receive and pass back the fire orders and when at the latter I was only too happy to sink into a deep sleep before another rude awakening.

'Hey, wake up, wake up, it's your turn on duty again!'

On one occasion we drove up by jeep beyond Rauray to where the carrier was stationed behind a high bank. On the way up we had passed the damaged carrier of another troop of our regiment. It had gone over a mine, turned upside down by the force of the explosion and trapped the signaller underneath. The OP officer had been thrown clear with the radio operator and both had been slightly wounded but the OP assistant who was the driver had been killed. The signaller who had been trapped beneath was now clear and told of his experience. As he was a tall man he had been lucky to have escaped without injury.

As night fell a Nebelwerfer opened up sending its

"whooping" cry into the skies. The mortar bombs fell in front by a chateau which was illuminated by the explosions. The troop commander tried to get a bearing on the enemy weapon and brought down a Mike Target where he suspected it to be. As the order to fire was given I saw the sky to the rear lit by a line of orange flashes, heard the shells whine overhead and their explosion somewhere in front which co-incided with the rumble of the gunfire from whence they came.

It was not long before the "moaning minnie" fired again from a different position.

'The bugger's moved,' grumbled the troop commander, 'He's got the werfer on a truck and as soon as he fires he beetles off, sets up another target and fires again.'

The inability to pin-point the firing positions of mobile mortars led to the establishment of a special anti-mortar unit, but my involvement with that comes later in the campaign.

All night the British artillery opened up on selected targets from other units as well as our own. All night there was a long line of orange flashes, the whine of shells above and explosions in enemy territory. I was glad I was not a German facing such formidable bombardments.

Just before dawn a bombardment was concentrated on the chateau followed by an infantry advance. There was no opposition. The Germans had left the building and retreated to new positions in the treacherous bocage. The carrier was driven into the courtyard and carefully we entered the building. We were aware of the danger of booby traps. Open a door unsuspectingly and a carefully placed grenade could explode killing or maiming the leading entrant. Climb through a window, trip over a wire stretched across the floor and an anti-tank rocket (a bazooka or panzerfaust) could blast across the room. But here there were no booby-traps. We made our way into a cellar which had been occupied by the enemy a few hours before. The troop commander kicked over the dirty mattresses and remnants of tinned food.

'I'm not using this place until it has been disinfected,' he said, 'Call up on the radio for a couple of cans of Lysol to be sent up.'

He set up his observation post on a top storey looking out of a broken wall to the formal gardens and the bocage beyond. The carrier was pulled close into the wall of the house and an extension lead passed up for the radio. My fellow signaller remained on duty with the officer and his assistant and I looked around some of the rooms in the chateau. Pictures hung askew on the walls of the rooms and bricks and dust covered the floor and furniture. It seemed sacrilege to destroy such a beautiful home and I wondered who had lived there and where they were now. I picked up an envelope lying on the floor and stuffed it into my pocket against the day when I could make out its writing and find out our location. It was the chateau of Fontenoy-le-Mesnil. The jeep arrived with the disinfectant and I was given the task of cleaning out the cellar. The fear that our troop commander had was of lice and the attendant possibility of contracting typhus. Some German soldiers had become lousy, and none of us wanted to emulate them. When Naples had been captured in 1943 typhus had broken out due to the breakdown of sanitation and the British Army was prepared for similar epidemics in France. I had been on an anti-typhus course in Norfolk several months before the invasion and was one of six men in the regiment trained to deal with lice detection and their irradication.

The cellar disinfected I reported to the troop commander who viewed it with evident distaste.

'I still don't like it. I'm not going to take any risks. We'll go back to the hedgerow where we were last night.'

And so we went.

5

The move to Demouville

Towards the end of July we received the order to move. It was to be a night move so as to keep it a secret from the enemy. Only the senior officers knew where we were going. The quads were driven up from the wagon lines, the guns were pulled from their well established pits. The radio trucks were loaded and the command post abandoned. Our home for several weeks was to be left. We felt a mixture of regret, foreboding and curiosity.

Regret at leaving the familiar surroundings, foreboding over our future movements and curiosity to see just what was to lie round the corner. We had been relatively secure in our apple orchard and we had dug well in. Apart from the first day when the gun position was almost over-run no enemy retaliation had been taken against our battery.

Dennis, George and I dismantled the dug out, rolled up our blankets, wrapped them in our ground sheets and stowed them away in the trucks.

'We had a good place here,' said George.

'I don't fancy digging another one all over again,' remarked Dennis. 'Tonight we have to sleep by our vehicles in the next orchard where 384 Battery have been,' I added.

That night a German battery shelled our former gun position and a shell exploded at the mouth of our former dug out. Another landed in the centre of the abandoned command post. Others exploded where some of our guns had been. In the morning we surveyed the damage.

'Weren't we the lucky ones!'

In the dusk of that day the regiment moved off in convoy. Each vehicle followed the tiny light glimmering on the rear of the one in front. It was a long and arduous journey. As GBA bumped and swayed its way through the night I was certain that much of our journey was across rough country. There were many stops. Each time the truck started off there were creaks and groans from the body work as the heavily laden Bedford lurched forward on uneven ground.

As dawn broke we halted in a scene of utter desolation. Our troop deployed in an area that had once been cornfields. It was now a wasteland. On every side were bomb and shell craters and muddy earth churned deep by tank tracks. The debris of war was strewn about. A knocked out German anti-tank gun, a twisted metal tank track, a steel helmet pierced by a bullet, tattered remains of uniform and the smell of death.

To the left was a copse of poplar trees, badly shredded by shell fire. To the far right was the ruins of a village: Demouville. Ahead the wasteland stretched away for a mile or more until a line of devastated trees could be seen. To the rear was more wasteland and then a dusty road that had led us to our position.

Immediately all available men began to dig in. Camouflage netting appeared over the guns. In the course of the day several targets were called and the guns went into action.

Tiffy was called over more than once to fix a fault.

'Tiffy, the buffer oil is leaking.'

'Tiffy, the breech block has jammed.'

Lieutenant Cannell and his staff felt uneasy about the position. It was so open, so vulnerable. This view was also shared by some of the gun crews. More than one of the gun sergeants came across to the command post and asked if the troop could move nearer to the trees. The battery commander listened to the requests but declined.

'Everyone has had a tiring time. We don't want to move again and have to dig more gun pits,' said Major Draper as he returned to the battalion headquarters of the heavily depleted Wellingtons.

I strolled over to No 2 gun where Dougie Marshall and Johnny Feaver, a former mate of mine, were manning the gun. Dougie was the gun layer, a bombardier.

'When I get back home to Leeds,' said Dougie in his gravelly voice, 'When I get back to Leeds I won't cross the bloody road unless somebody holds my hand.'

I returned to the command post and took up duty on the radio. Five minutes later there was the whine of incoming shells and a concentration of high explosives rained upon the gun position. Fred Dalton appeared in the entrance and flung himself on the floor. We waited a few seconds. Yes, here came some more. A second group of shells exploded all around. Earth was scattered every where. The canvas roof was torn away. We had not had time to build very deep nor make ourselves a decent roof. There was the smell of exploded shell burst and then a silence that hung seemingly long in the air. No more came.

A cry came up, 'No 2 gun has been hit!'

My duty was to remain where I was on the set. Others raced to see what had happened. Piece by piece I got the news. Dougie Marshall and Johnny Feaver had been killed. Penhaligon, the taciturn Cornish driver of a quad, had been seriously wounded. The netting around No 2 gun was on fire. Several shell cases in the gun pit had exploded. The other guns and gunners were unhurt though badly shaken.

Not long after, the Major ordered a move that brought most of the troop within cover of the poplars and the digging in began all over again. But everyone felt happier in that new position.

If only the troop had been deployed there in the first place, we thought. Hunches are not always proved to be wrong.

Our position was some five miles west of Caen on the road to Troarn. It had been the scene of fierce fighting not long before. Wave upon wave of British and American bombers had pulverised the enemy positions to be followed by intensive artillery bombardment and a tank assault. The British had expected to move forward without too much opposition after such a bombardment, but once our forces advanced they came under concentrated German tank fire that destroyed many British tanks and slowed the advance to a crawl. As so often the Germans had dug in their superior tanks, ensured that their infantry was kept in deep shelters to emerge relatively unscathed, if deafened, to meet the onslaught of advancing troops.

Our division was now holding the ground won and our guns were in the middle of the earlier battlefield. The area was under direct enemy observation and any obvious move that we made was liable to bring down artillery fire.

There was frequent enemy shelling in reply to our own, but none fell in the wooded area. The German guns appeared to be ranged on to our former exposed position. It was never a happy place and I never felt at ease whilst we were there. We were ordered not to sleep more than two in a dug out and George and I proceeded to dig deep. I seem to remember that Dennis felt left out and dug a single hole for himself. This, our second underground home, was to be an improvement on the first. The semi-sandy soil, was easy to work in. We built two steps at right angles to our sleeping places and dug a shelf on each side for our belongings. There was plenty of timber to be found amongst the trees or to be plundered from the ruins of Demouville. This was used to make a strong roof which was covered with turf and soil. We felt quite secure in our little nest and free from the uneasy feeling when above ground in that gloomy terrain. The only snag were the mosquitoes. It was a hot August and the "mossies" swarmed and flew amongst us in the night like tiny hostile aircraft. Some of our companions declared that they feared the "mossies" more than the Luftwaffe. Some of the men were badly bitten and their arms and legs swelled up alarmingly. George and I did not suffer from bad bites but those we had itched and the little beasts tormented us especially when we were trying to sleep below ground. The troop was sent up anti-mosquito cream to keep the tiny tormentors at bay but the repellant seemed to some of us to be more effective as an attractor!

Another and more dangerous irritant was a large calibre gun that fired at targets indicated by dust thrown up by passing vehicles. This enemy gun was probably mounted on a railway wagon which was kept hidden in a railway tunnel when not actually firing. The shell or rocket fired had some kind of a booster charge that exploded in mid air, so that first one heard a loud "boom" in the sky followed by a large "bang" when it landed. It never engaged our gun position as a target but usually fired over us to unknown destinations further back.

One evening soon after our move to the shelter of the poplars George and I made our way carefully to Demouville to find extra pieces of wood to enhance the protection of our shelter. Several others came with us bent on a similar errand. It was an eerie scene with the smell of burning and dust pervading the air. Armed with suitable pieces of timber we crossed a road to the edge of another gun position and came across Maurice Tyerman, his head sticking out of a fox hole.

'Hello, Maurice, didn't expect to find you here.'

'Get back to your billet, lads,' uttered Maurice, 'This is no place to be walking around in at dusk. If Jerry doesn't get you the mosquitoes will.'

'Yes, we know. We lost two of our gun crew a couple of days ago. Take care, old son, watch out for those moaning minnies.'

That night as we lay in our newly re-inforced shelter we heard the "zoom-zoom" of an aircraft passing slowly overhead to be followed almost immediately by the whistle of a stick of bombs and the roar of the explosions as they detonated some three hundred yards behind us. The next night an enemy aircraft arrived at almost the same time and once more unloaded its bombs somewhere around us. Lieutenant Small, who had watched both events from outside the command post, came up with a theory.

'When Jerry comes over his lines the troops on the ground fire a white flare to show that he is now passing over them and on to our side. He waits a bit to find a target then makes his bombing run and we seem to get it. Now if I fire a white flare tonight when the 'plane comes over I'll confuse them and they'll go much further back and bomb somebody else!'

That night Lieutenant Small climbed to the top of a burnt out tank and as the enemy aircraft reverberated over he fired a white flare. Immediately the aircraft released its stick of bombs and brought the enterprising officer down from the tank much quicker than he had climbed up. No one appeared to be hurt. Only Lieutenant Small's dignity suffered.

'They must have changed the colour of the flare,' he said, But he did not repeat his ruse.

During this period I began to suffer from tooth-ache and my gum became swollen and painful. I was aware of an unpleasant discharge in my mouth. Reluctantly I decided to report sick. Two days later I found myself waiting at the road side for a regimental truck to pick me up and take me to the field hospital. The truck came slowly along the road careful not to raise any dust.

I clambered aboard and shared the drive with two other soldiers reporting sick. We did not speak as I recall. We had nothing to talk about and in any case the noise of the truck made any conversation difficult. The vehicle drove away from the shelter of the trees and on to the open road towards Couverille. A large sign at the road side proclaimed DUST MEANS DEATH. I began to feel I would prefer toothache to a final end to all pain. Our driver crawled along obeying the message of the sign. We passed another with a minor change in lettering, DUST BRINGS DEATH.

At last we moved behind a screen of trees and turned into a large meadow. The menace of dust was over. There were several big tents emblazoned with large red crosses on the canvas roofs. I was directed down a path through the meadow to a collection of smaller tents where the army dental corps was operating. I was the only patient and was soon sitting in the dentist's chair being examined. My experience of the military dentists had been good so far. I had been given two first rate crowns and had had some carefully executed fillings with the minimum of pain. Something I had not always had in civilian life. But here in a field in Normandy? It would not necessarily be the same.

As the dentist bent over me, a white coat pulled casually over his captain's uniform, there was sound of the air burst of the long range gun and the crump as the heavy shell exploded some way away. Someone was raising dust!

'You have rather a bad abscess,' said the dentist, quietly. 'I should really give you gas to take the tooth out but I don't have any right now. I'll have to give you a couple of injections and then pull it out. Or to be on the safe side you could come back in three days time when I shall have some gas, Jerry willing, of course.'

I said I would rather have it taken out now. I did not fancy repeating the danger of the dusty drive and in addition I did not know when the troop might be called upon to move.

'Right-ho then. I'll pull it out now. It should be all right. I'll give you some tablets to take to counter any infection. Should you have further trouble report sick again.'

The needle was inserted to the front of the tooth and again to the back. I was left for a few moments for the anaesthetic to work. Once more the long range enemy gun boomed and cracked. This time the shell landed a little nearer. Not on an incoming ambulance, I hoped.

Back came my dentist and the tooth was easily removed. I had felt no pain. I spat blood into the rinsing bowl. I arose a little unsteadily to my feet.

'Take these tablets for a week. They should prevent any infection.'

I returned the way I had come lurching from side to side in the bumpy truck hoping that the driver was being even more careful than before. He was. No shells came in our direction and soon I was back at the gun position. I took my tablets, and felt much better with the poisoned tooth removed. There were no ill effects.

It was while we were at Demouville that we were introduced to a new food. It was tinned pudding that was hot, moistened by its own chocolate sauce and divided into three portions. One portion per man. We all thought it delicious and George called it "nightmare duff" because you had such dreams anticipating the next time it was to arrive. The name "nightmare duff" spread through the troop and beyond and became a household word.

'We got "nightmare duff" today?' the gunners would call out to the cooks as they prepared to dish out the food. The cooks did not at first understand and would get angry until the meaning was explained to them and they carried the information back to the wagon lines and, who knows, back to the colonel himself.

George was quite a wit and a good and cheerful companion. Once in the dug-out in the middle of the afternoon when both of us were catching up on lost sleep, George observed me sitting up, taking off my glasses and cleaning them. I was, in fact fast asleep when I did this. When I woke up George asked me if I was cleaning my glasses in order to see my dreams better! This wisecrack soon got around the camp and I was subjected to some good natured leg-pulling.

At the end of the second week it was decided that the 3 ton trucks used for ammunition carrying could be spared to take detachments of soldiers back to the beach at Lion-sur-Mer for a day's rest and relaxation. I was lucky enough to be chosen to go on the first day trip. With others from the troop we rolled carefully across the DUST BRINGS DEATH area until clear of enemy observation and then bowled along through the countryside to the sea. Lion-sur-Mer was a small seaside resort. Bungalows lined the coast road and there were several cafes in the town.

The vehicles parked in a field by the beach and we all jumped out.

'Do not go on the beach,' were the orders given, 'You can go along the grass, on the road and into the village. No looting.'

It was wonderful to sit on the grass, look at the sea, strip off some clothing, lie back, relax and feel safe. It was wonderful too, to walk along the coast road, peer into the deserted and shuttered bungalows and their gardens and feel once more the glimmer of holidays by the sea. We found a cafe open and went in. The only thing to buy was cheese. There were round boxes of Camembert cheese but nothing else. So we bought some boxes of Camembert, sat on the steps of the cafe and ate the cheese, peeling off the silver paper and juggling the pieces in our fingers. It tasted real. It tasted good. The sun shone and we stripped to the waist and sunbathed. Then it was time to climb back into the trucks and be driven back to the gun position. For several days detachments left for the beach to enjoy themselves. Then the pleasure stopped. Someone had walked on a landmine in the field where the trucks were driven and had been killed. Upon further inspection more mines were found. So the holiday by the sea came to an untimely end and many of us counted our luck once more.

Inevitably my turn came to man the forward OP carrier. The front was quiet. The main battle was raging south of us. We could hear the rumble of gunfire; see the bombers flying over and hear the crump of bombs.

The carrier was parked near the railway at Troarn. The observation post itself was in a farmyard in what had been a pig-sty. The signal wire had been run out to a handset located there. I do not remember seeing any of our infantry. For some reason which I cannot recall I was located in the abandoned pig-sty on my own. My duty was to observe and report any sign of enemy movement. It was a scorchingly hot day. I had carried up my rations of biscuit, margarine and jam in an open mess tin. I became the attraction of many wasps. I spent most of my time on duty avoiding the direct rays of the sun and keeping the wasps out of the jam. I had never been particularly afraid of wasps and my four hour experience in the pig-sty taught me not to be afraid at all. In the end the wasps won their battle to possess my jam and I ended up eating dry biscuit. But I had one victory I was not stung though they swarmed around me constantly. Perhaps the anti-mosquito cream kept them off me. Perhaps it was really anti-wasp cream!

The day came when we had orders to advance. Hearts were high as we began to realise that the effective breakout from the enlarged beachhead was at last happening. Those terrible bocage battles where so many thousands of men had died and even more had been wounded to gain a mile or less of enemy held territory were about to end. Jerry was beaten and on the run. The German 7th Army was trapped between the closing pincers of British and American forces and being forced to flee eastwards through the Falaise Gap. The task of our division was to move eastwards through wooded countryside to the River Seine, flushing out the enemy wherever he could be found.

At first every time we moved we dug in. After two moves in one day and the onset of darkness every man was exhausted even though the soil was an easily dug sand. I sat in the hastily dug command post, earphones on head, signal pad on lap, cigarette in hand — and fell fast asleep. I was awakened by the sardonic tones of the GPO assistant.

'You've set yourself on fire, you silly bugger. Hey! Wake up. You're on fire'

I awoke in a daze. What was happening? What was he

saying?

I leapt to my feet with a scream. My cigarette had burned a hole in my denim trousers and the smouldering hole was becoming an ever widening circle. The pain of the burn on my leg rendered me wide awake. That was the second time I had fallen asleep on duty.

'You have a habit of going to sleep when you are supposed to be awake,' glowered the assistant.

'Well, I bloody soon woke up this time, didn't I?' I retorted with some asperity.

After the next move and with no sign of retaliation from the enemy, those who could crashed out in a barn filled with sweet smelling hay. Oh, how blissful it was to fall into a deep, deep sleep without the danger of disturbance. In the morning as we pulled on our boots and stood up there was a cry,

'We've got red spiders all over us!'

It was true. Everyone who had bedded down in the hay was covered with tiny mites. They were red and very active, enjoying the exploration of our clothes and tracking back and forth over our bodies. They did not seem to sting (at least they did not sting me), but they gave a nasty itching feeling.

With cries of alarm and disgust we all vacated the barn and stripped off our clothes to shake them clear of the red invaders. They had to be shaken and shaken. The tiny insects just did not want to leave. For several days afterwards we all felt that we had some of them still with us and we were often right for our blankets proved more difficult to clean out than our clothes. We vowed that never again would we sleep in a barn full of hay however sweet smelling.

We passed on through the town of Mezidon, stopping once to go into action against a lone 88mm gun that was pinning down our advance. The German 88mm was a versatile weapon that could be used as a tank gun, a field gun and an anti-aircraft gun. Mounted in a Tiger or a Panther it could out-gun any of our tanks, and it was readily admitted by our tank crews that it usually took three of our tanks to knock out one of the German giants. As a field gun it could fire high explosive shells or armour piercing. As an anti-aircraft gun it was the major weapon used by the FLAK Regiments to defend the Third Reich.

Its sound was distinctive. Being a high velocity gun the shell travelled at great speed so that the sound of the gun firing and the roar of the exploding shell were almost simultaneous.

It made a sharp noise like "crack-bump" and if you were the target there was never any time to take cover at the commencement of shelling. We all learned to respect the 88mm and to fear it. Our 25-pounders on the other hand were gun-howitzers with much lower muzzle velocity. The shells could have a fairly low trajectory if firing at a low angle. But they could also be fired to lob a shell high in the air to come down on top of an enemy position. This the 88mm could not do. As a consequence the two sides used their artillery differently. The 88mm was a brilliant all-rounder but in the field it was dispersed to defend crossroads and strong points. The 25-pounder was deployed in troops and batteries and regiments to bring down dispersed or concentrated fire as required. Because of the highly developed radio communication system it was possible to link up many guns on one target and then shortly afterwards to revert to troop targets. The Mike Target was the combination used most in the campaign in North Western Europe and many of the enemy troops that were captured believed that our guns were electrically controlled. They were in the sense that the air waves were used to transmit fire orders but wrong in the sense that the guns themselves were electrically linked in some way. Certainly the Germans were out gunned throughout the campaign.

At one place when we stopped in pasture land there were dead cows lying in the field. One of gun numbers who had been an apprentice butcher offered to cut out some fresh meat and cook it on a cordite fire helped out by twigs and dry leaves. There were those who were sceptical believing that the meat would be tough and in any case undesirable. There were also those who longed for some fresh meat and were willing to have a taste.

After some time hacking at a piece of leg with an unsuitable knife the "butcher" carried the meat across to the fire and aided by willing mates proceeded to roa[illegible] it. Visions of Robin Hood and his Merry Men flashed befo[illegible] us. At last the meat was considered ready and we gathered round to share in the meal. The cow meat proved inedible. It was as tough as an old boot and had as much flavour as leather anklets! The sceptics had been right.

The next day we were into the forests bordering the Seine and found at the roadside a great discovery. George and Dennis went into the woods to fulfil the needs of nature and came back dancing with glee.

'Look what we've found! A dump of German tinned food.'

It was true. There were tins and tins of lard and tins and tins of pork abandoned just inside the woods. There were also several frying pans and other cooking utensils made of aluminium. A large frying pan and several armfuls of mixed tins were appropriated by George and Dennis to be hidden in George's jeep.

'We don't want the stuff in GBA because Cannell will claim it all.'

As if gifted with second sight the Liverpuddlian voice of the Lieutenant was heard. 'Tiffy, what have you got there?'

Trust him to spot what had been found! One could no more keep a secret about anything that might add to his comfort than keep a secret from oneself! We smiled behind his back at his strong sense of self-preservation, yet we admired his competence as a gunnery officer. The discovery was revealed and the Lieutenant's batman was sent to collect a rightful share. Soon the good news reached the nearest gun crews as they leapt out of their quads and stretched their legs. Before long there were several camp fires burning and the smell of cooking fat frying. Numerous hungry soldiers enjoyed a tasty meal that evening.

'What we need now,' exclaimed George, 'are some spuds and then we can have some chips.'

Ham and chips at Jerry's expense. How wonderful! But the potatoes were not so easily come by and had to wait until we had crossed the Seine and lost our cooks at the same time. The problem all the advancing troops had was how to get over the Seine. There was talk of a bridge at Pont Audemer, but when we reached it it turned out to be a bridge over a lesser river. So we continued to drive eastwards not stopping to engage any targets but going as fast as we could to cross the Seine at Rouen. Just outside that city we had to stop for a day because of the pressure of troop traffic on the available routes. It was here that we encountered for the first time men of the French Resistance. They emerged from the woods and greeted us warmly. They were dressed in motley attire, the only common means of identification being an armband with the letters FFI.

They were doing a great job clearing the retreating and disorganised stragglers of the Wehrmacht out of the woods and forcing them to surrender or be killed. The Germans were abandoning masses of equipment: tanks without petrol, guns, vehicles, horses and supplies of very kind. They travelled by night as far as possible to avoid air attack. Fighter bombers roared overhead from time to time and rocket firing Typhoons roamed the skies looking for travelling convoys. We had come across burnt out vehicles with charred bodies inside, but had not seen any living enemy. At the side of the road we frequently saw a stick with a bundle of straw crudely tied to it marking the site of fox hole into which cover could be taken in the event of air assault.

The orders were received to come through Rouen. It had been heavily bombed by the RAF and many of the roads were impassable on account of fallen masonry. As so often happened in this campaign the efforts to destroy the enemy and prevent his movements had the effect of preventing the movements of our own troops as well. We could not get through the city before some streets had been cleared by army bulldozers. Eventually we reached the road bridge across the Seine to find it down. We were then directed to the foot of the railway bridge which had been blown in several places. It was, however, considered possible to drive across it. The centre section was just at water level. The engineers who were manning the bridge told us to drive very slowly. We drove across the bridge bumping over sleepers and twisted rails. It was easy for the carriers with their caterpillar tracks, not too difficult for the quads with their large wheels and powerful engines even though they were hauling a gun limber each, but it required great skill to move the heavily laden 15cwt radio trucks over the uneven way. I got out and walked with Fred Dalton to save weight and we jumped from sleeper to sleeper as the tidal water flowed swiftly a foot below. At the centre span the rails were a few inches under water and as the vehicles bumped along the span shook and fell further below the water level.

'Keep going, keep going!' shouted the engineers at the end of the span. At last GBA was over and we drew up on the new bank and waited for the guns to cross. They came slowly and cautiously over the precarious bridge followed by George in his ubiquitous jeep.

'It won't last much longer,' confided an engineer officer to Lieutenant Cannell. 'Once the tide turns and comes up the river from the sea in full flood the bridge will go.'

Not long after as we slowly ascended the river hill to the east of the ancient town we looked back and saw the centre section collapse, carrying with it three ammunition wagons belonging to the Polish Armoured Division (so we were told). Our ammunition wagons and our cooks' wagons were left behind on the other side and they did not manage to rejoin us for three days during which time we lived on our German tins and potatoes lifted from the farmers' fields.

6

The assault on Le Havre

Once across the Siene the 49th Infantry Division was placed under the command of the Canadian 1st Army whose appointed task was to capture the Channel ports of Le Havre, Dieppe, Boulogne and Calais. Of this Army the 1st Corps comprising 49th and 51st Highland Divisions were given the task of capturing the big port and industrial city of Le Havre. The assault under the code name Operation Astonia was planned to begin on Sunday, September 10th.

Le Havre was heavily fortified against attack from the sea. The landward defences were incomplete but considerable minefields had been laid and a deep anti-tank ditch had been dug. Many concrete underground forts, called bunkers, and concrete pill boxes had been constructed with interlocking fields of fire for anti-tank guns and machine guns. These were supported by field guns and anti-aircraft guns of various calibres. The defence of Le Havre was entrusted to Colonel Eberhard Wildermuth. He was not a regular soldier but had wide experience of battle. He commanded a garrison of some 12,000 men made up from many units. There was a fortress cadre and a security regiment which had been defending the port against a long awaited naval attack and there were elements of many Wehrmacht forces which had retreated into Le Havre and had been hastily organised into defensive companies. As one German officer was to say later, 'We could have held out for weeks had we had properly organised and equipped troops.'

Of all this I was supremely ignorant as the Bren carrier in which I was now travelling arrived at a farm a few miles from the city and one mile from the leading enemy positions. Captain Thompson had returned from his convalescence in England and had promptly reorganised his OP staff. All was very quiet. There had been a flurry of excitement the day before when Sergeant Eddie Gawler's gun crew had driven straight into a group of German soldiers going along a lane to Le Havre in the same direction. In the advance the guns were sometimes ahead of the OP and the infantry. The Germans had halted, turned their anti-tank gun around and begun to prepare to open fire. The British gun crew had also halted and had feverishly unlimbered the 25-pounder to face the enemy 100 yards down the road. The Germans got a round off first. It was armour piercing and swished viciously over the heads of the toiling British. Sergeant Gawler had to get his quad out of the line of fire before the reply could be fired. The quad driver sweated and strained at the wheel to get the vehicle off the road and out of the way, only too well aware that the next enemy shot was most likely to tear into him. But the enemy did not fire again. It was their turn to work desperately at taking their gun out of action and beating a hasty retreat. By the time Gawler had given the order "Fire!" the enemy were rounding the bend in the lane and the shell flew into the hedgerow sending up clods of earth and pieces of vegetation.

'We've got too far ahead,' stated the gun sergeant rather obviously to a surprised and shaken crew The quad drove round with some difficulty, the gun was limbered up once more and the unit retreated down the lane until they met another gun crew coming along. They both waited for further orders before venturing any further toward Le Havre.

All was very quiet along the now established front. The guns were dug in and waiting for something to happen. To our rear could be heard the rumble of tanks. There was the occasional sound of a motorbike being driven through the gear box. There was no sign of life from the German side.

There had been heavy rain the day before our arrival. My companions and I had slept in a ditch that during the night had slowly filled with water. Fortunately we had placed our ground sheets beneath us but the water saturated them and splashed over the edges to soak our blankets. I experienced sleep on a water bed long before it had been designed for patients in hospital! My blankets remained damp for a fortnight despite attempts to dry them out over the engine of the carrier.

During our second day at the farm Captain Thompson took the carrier out on a reconnoitre. I was on the radio keeping in touch with the gun position. After a journey along the edge of several fields during which time the captain stopped several times to survey the terrain through his field glasses, he had the carrier driven up a steep hill in full view of the enemy. How slowly the carrier ground its way up the slope! Any moment we expected the enemy to open fire and hear the "crump, crump" of shells bursting around us or the sharp burst of machine gun fire raking across the open top. But nothing happened. The only noise was that of the carrier's engine roaring away in its lowest gear.

'Jerry doesn't want to give his positions away,' shouted Captain Thompson as we breasted the hill.

But as we turned safely down the reverse slope, I realised clearly that the climb had been the purpose of that reconnoitre in order to try to attract enemy fire so that enemy firing positions could be spotted and plotted. But the Germans were not going to give their positions away. These would have to be discovered in the heat of battle.

Sunday, September 10th, dawned bright and turned warm: a really beautiful day in early Autumn. During the early afternoon infantry and tanks began to form up in strength. Our carrier moved up close to the command carrier of a company of the 2nd Battalion of the Gloucesters. Around 4 o'clock we heard the roar of aircraft and saw and heard a host of RAF bombers pulverise the enemy positions across the open fields before us.

Our own guns opened up to join in the bombardment. For what seemed like an hour wave after wave of bombers (there were 400 Halifaxes and Lancasters used) came over dropping their heavy bombs. Huge clouds of black smoke and dust engulfed the enemy, pierced by huge orange and red flashes. The artillery of the entire Corps added to the onslaught. The noise was deafening and the ground shook even though the nearest point of impact was more than 1,200 yards away. Surely no German soldier could be left after such a barrage?

The aerial bombardment ceased. The last of the giant four engined bombers rumbled away. It did not seem that any had been shot down despite the anti-aircraft fire and the low level of their approach. Perhaps their low level had hampered the ground defence. At a signal the flail tanks of 79th Division (known as the "Funnies" because of their specialised equipment) moved forward ready to beat the suspected minefields with their circling chains, followed by other tanks and infantry. The guns maintained their bombardment. Some of the tanks were flame throwers towing trailers carrying their deadly liquid. Some of the tanks carried huge mortar bombs like sinister toffee apples ready to be discharged at enemy pill boxes. Others were designed to put down large piles of brushwood or bridges to enable the advancing forces to cross the anti-tank ditch. Yet more were conventional tanks with long and slender gun barrels prepared to take on enemy tanks or to destroy whatever was to be in their way.

As we moved forward I kept up a running commentary over the No 19 set to the Battery Commander who on such an important occasion had taken over the microphone and headset from his signaller in order to get as close as possible to the action.

'Hello Able Baker one, we are going forward at the speed of the infantry. Some German shells are landing among us — they are firing air burst over our heads. I can't tell if it's to range or whether to shower us with shrapnel. Able Baker two, over.'

The big black shell bursts overhead continued. Were they from big naval guns depressed to fire overland or were they from field guns? I never knew the answer to that question.

Several tanks had stopped either hit by armour piercing shells or having gone over a mine and blown a track. Here and there an infantryman staggered and fell, hit by shell fragments or small arms fire. We could not see where the enemy fire was coming from. The smoke and flame rendered such observation impossible. The noise of our massed artillery was continuous and we could hear our own shells whining overhead. The heat from the carrier's engine combined with heat from the sun made the sweat run. A dull chronic fear gripped my stomach.

After what seemed like hours our carrier reached the edge of the wide anti-tank ditch and prepared to cross the crude bridge that the tanks and assault engineers had put down. Two lines of white tape about ten feet apart showed us the way through the minefield. As we groped towards the bridge a carrier in front of us received a direct hit and a blanket roll was flung into the air to lodge in our tracks. Our carrier slewed round and stopped dead. Three of us jumped out to free the obstacle from the track while the driver started the engine again and let the gear into reverse and then into forward again. The track moved an inch and ground to a halt. Fearful lest he should burn the clutch out, the driver stopped engaging gear and waited for the offending blankets to be prised out. Other vehicles and foot soldiers crossed the minefield as we struggled and sweated and swore at the obstruction. Two knocked out Churchill tanks to our right partly served to protect us (I can remember that the machine gun in one of them was firing at an unseen target all the time) and partly to block our access to the cleared path through the minefield. It was gathering dusk when the carrier was finally freed and we slithered along between the white tapes barely keeping within their confines. But where were our protecting infantry? How could we give them gunnery help if we could not find the company commander? The dusk was illuminated by a burning building in the near distance. The driver pulled the carrier under the protection of a bank surmounted by trees. It was like being in the bocage again. Beyond lay an orchard. Captain Thompson waited for a while expecting to be contacted by the infantry and to be told when the orchard was cleared of the enemy. No one came. We seemed to be deserted. Later we learned that the company commander had been killed. The noise of battle diminished and almost died away. It became dark. The guns fell silent, only the intermittent burst of machine gun fire could be heard.

A calm fell upon the carrier. I felt grateful to be alive: a wave of utter weariness came over me and with my headset buzzing and crackling in my ears I was on the point of dozing off.

Then, incredibly, a German helmet appeared over the side of the carrier.

'Hande hoch!' cried the enemy. I raised my hands. We were surrounded by a German patrol. I was motioned to get out, and clambered over the side. My captor fumbled to turn the set off but failed to master the controls so he contented himself with dismantling the aerial connection. I watched in a daze. It would not take a minute to get the set working again.

With hands on head we were prodded and pushed to the other side of the bank and made to sit on the grass. Any attempt to ease our hands from head incurred an instant command and a sharp prod with a rifle.

A young Lieutenant came up with Captain Thompson, guarding him with a Luger pistol.

'I tried to give —' began the troop commander, but he was silenced by a push in the back with the pistol.

'Englander? Canadaien?' the lieutenant asked. He wore the white insignia of the infantry.

'Ich Englander,' I replied.

'Gut, Canada nicht gut. Sie toten gefangenen.'

I engaged him in my halting schoolboy German. He was 19 years old, two years younger than I. He came from Hamburg. He was in the infantry. It seemed that Captain Thompson had been grabbed first as he was making a recce into the orchard. He had called out to us but no one had heard him. The German officer had a dozen men with him. We sat uneasily on the ground waiting for the next move. What was going to happen to us? It all seemed unreal, as if it were happening to someone else. I felt no fear, just fatigue and mild interest. Then we heard our artillery opening up and the shells crashing the other side of the bank. Captor and captive alike flung themselves on to the ground as close to the protective bank as possible. British face was pressed into German jackboot; German hands clung to British feet. There was another salvo of fire followed by another. Fortunately none of the shells burst our side of the bank. Then it was all over.

'Raus, raus!' cried the lieutenant. We got up and sorted ourselves out, the distinction between captor and captive being firmly established once more. In single file, closely guarded, we made our way down a sloping field. The darkness was total with no moon or stars to be seen, but an occasional shell burst or star shell lit the sky momentarily. To our right behind our lines flashes from artillery glowed orange and red. As we trudged along I dug in my pockets and found my artillery code which I tore up and dropped bit by bit as I went. It would have been of little use to the enemy but it was the least that I could do as an act of defiance. No German would have the satisfaction of opening it and reading STRICTLY CONFIDENTIAL. I also dropped some French francs. Did anyone ever find them afterwards I wonder and spend them?

As we went along German soldiers were collected from their fox holes. There was obviously a general retreat to other defensive positions. The procession now much lengthened reached a footpath and turned left down a steep hillside. Trees could be seen overhead in the darkness. By now searchlights were shining straight paths of light from behind our lines. We called this "Monty's Moonlight" and it was used to provide some light and direction for our troops to advance by. We came under further fire from the small calibre Bofors guns that were being used to give direction to our tanks moving forward. The shells were tracers forming broken lines of light and landing and exploding all around our column. I stood foolishly still thinking somehow that these explosions being from our own anti-aircraft guns could not do me any injury. The Germans had no such illusions and took cover in all directions. Under the cover of the dark and confusion our carrier driver, Wilf Smith, slipped away and eventually made his way back to the carrier and drove it back to the gun position. For this he was later awarded the Military Medal, which he thoroughly deserved on account of his initiative. It never occurred to me to try to escape. I was thinking that the war was over for me and that I should be spending the next few months in a prisoner of war camp. Then I thought that I would be under air attack from our own planes and having seen earlier that afternoon what could be in store for me I began to wish that I too had made a getaway.

All these thoughts had whizzed through my mind in a matter of seconds and I came to the surface to find myself diving for cover as the Bofors shells exploded close by.

The shelling stopped and the Germans began to form the prisoners up and to count us. They realised that one was missing and began to search around growing more and more angry. But they could not find the missing bombardier and finally gave up and the party moved forward. Soon the line of soldiers reached a huge underground bunker. Captain Thompson, Jim Pearce and I were pushed into the command post which was lit by several powerful oil lamps. Jim and I were stood against a wall whilst the captain was interrogated by the senior German officer.

Hauptman Kurt Langner of the 86th Alpine Division was a regular Wehrmacht officer. He was dressed immaculately as if straight from a Hollywood film set. He wore the Iron Cross, a Russian Campaign strip and epaulettes. His boots were highly polished and there was a display of heel-clicking and Heil Hitler's as we were handed over. He rang his superior officer on a field telephone on the wall.

'Wir haben ein funkwagon gefunden,' he reported.

Captain Thompson made little response to the questions that were asked of him and when offered wine and food he refused. I did the same when asked, as did Jim. We felt that we had better be British together. There were several doctors in the room dressed in green surgical gowns and with operating masks beneath their chins. The gowns were blood-stained. The German officer's batman was a tall gefreite (corporal) who was also wearing the Russian Campaign stripe and was obviously devoted to his superior. Suddenly there was a commotion in the doorway. Three elderly looking German soldiers were bundled in, looking terrified, and a feltwebel (sergeant) gave Captain Langner to understand that they had left their posts during the attack. Langner stood in front of each of them in turn, clicked his heels, slapped their faces on both cheeks, tore off their campaign colours, removed their leather belts with storm torches attached to them and told them to get against the wall were Jim and I were standing.

'Nien,' he yelled, after a moments thought. 'You are dishonourable. These English are honourable prisoners! Stand away from them — into the cupboard with you.'

And so these three luckless men were bundled into what looked like a broom cupboard!

After a short while Jim and I were taken deep into the bunker to sit in a dank passageway guarded by the tall corporal who took out his Luger and threatened us with it whenever we moved. Meanwhile our troop commander was led away by Hauptman Langner into his private room where they spent a more comfortable night, apparently drinking the last of his champagne.

As we sat in the smelly and draughty passage we saw many German soldiers who were wounded lying on bunks and being attended to by doctors and orderlies. One orderly bundled some poor soldier out of the underground ward shouting, 'Raus, raus!' and raining kicks and blows on him. Later in the night we were joined by one of our foot soldiers who had been picked up by another patrol. Three French girls came out of another room and joined us to talk. They remonstrated with me over the bombing of civilians in Le Havre and the heavy casualties that had been inflicted. I tried to tell them that I was sorry but it was war and pointed out how indiscriminately the Germans had bombed London. Whether it was my poor French or the weakness of my case, I do not know, but they went away as angry as they had come. Had they been sleeping with their German boyfriends or merely taking shelter in the bunker? Did it matter anyway? The corporal was glad to see them go as he had been agitated by the conversation that he had not been able to understand. All this time the noise of battle had recommenced and was now drawing nearer. There was no pause between the salvoes as a creeping barrage came closer to the bunker. Dawn broke and dimly lit the passage. There was a cry from Captain Thompson who emerged into the passage way.

'Come on, it's all over. The Jerries have decided to surrender to us!'

Bewildered we stood up and the tall corporal looked uncertain.

'I have persuaded Hauptman Langner that it is his duty

as a German officer to surrender for the sake of the wounded.'

At the other end of the passage the German captain was expostulating to the young lieutenant and other soldiers. Those who wished to continue the fight were to withdraw and leave Langner with the wounded and those who wished to surrender.

Not without ceremony the officers remaining gave up their pistols. Langner showed Thompson the position of the battalion headquarters and invited him to go there to take his commanding officer prisoner. Captain Thompson agreed and told us to guard the remaining Germans who by a reversal of fate had now become our prisoners.

Suddenly we were overwhelmed by them. They came to shake us by the hand, they produced photgraphs of their wives and sweethearts and children. One very rotund soldier exclaimed that now the war was over for him he would no longer be sent to the Russian front. Another said, pumping my hand, that he would be sent on a boat to Canada, and there would be lots of pretty girls there.

Having been at war with them for four years and prior to that having seen the menace of Hitler (I was no supporter of Chamberlain's appeasement policy in '38 and '39), and having endured air raids at home in which my father and uncle had been killed, and having, moreover, been conditioned by wartime propaganda, it was indeed difficult to take all this effusion of sentiment and comradeship from these men. To date, to me all German soldiers of whatever kind had been grey, hostile figures capable of ruthless behaviour. Brave, certainly, good fighters, yes, members of an efficient war machine, but not men with whom one wished to rub shoulders and become suddenly friendly.

We were wary. We backed away. We wanted to line them up and march them away. But where to and with what authority? I looked round for some kind of weapon. My Sten had been left in the carrier. I saw a Mauser rifle and picked it up. I motioned for them to put all their arms against the wall. They were delighted to obey. Having done so they returned to the hand grasping and photograph showing and back slapping. Once more we were overwhelmed. We felt we could be crushed against the wall.

We were rescued by Captain Thompson who had returned with Hauptman Langner dressed ceremoniously in his elegantly tailored greatcoat. The prisoners were lined up in the approach slope to the bunker and I was bidden to see if it was safe for the column to emerge. The barrage had stopped some half hour before. Cautiously I walked up the slope tying as I went a discarded tea towel which our Captain passed to me. It went on to the end of my newly acquired rifle to indicate the white flag of surrender. I peered round the parapet and made out some Scottish soldiers advancing cautiously up the track.

'I'm English,' I shouted, 'We've got some prisoners. Will you take them?'

All I got was a vigorous shake of the head and I was pointed back down the track. The advance section went past taking cover from behind every bush and as they skirmished forward the next section came up the lane.

I hailed them in a similar fashion.

The brawny sergeant said, 'Keep them yoursel.' We've got an important job to do. We can no be bothered wi' prisoners.' But I was luckier with the third wave.

'Bring 'em oot,' commanded a kilted sergeant, 'but take them back yoursel'. We have noo the time oursel.'

I dashed back to the assembled Germans who were looking apprehensive at the prospect of exposing themselves. Langner ordered them forward and led by him and Thompson with the faithful corporal in attendance the column commenced its journey out of the bunker. Jim guarded the centre and I brought up the rear. The column spilled across the lane, through the advancing Scots and back up the steep path that we had descended in the dark some eight hours earlier.

As the last of the column crossed the track they were stopped by some of the advancing infantry. They demanded watches and rings from the prisoners. I was angered. My sense of justice was outraged.

'Leave them alone. We were their prisoners and they treated us well. They didn't try and take our watches and rings.'

'If we don't take their valuables they'll be taken at the prison cage,' was the reply. I was hardly in a position to

Fountaine-la-Mallet — above, the site of the bunker in 1944 — now used as petrol dumps.

Below, here is where Captain Langer was killed on September, 11th 1944. These photos were taken on September 10th 1989, forty-five years after.

argue.

'There are German wounded and doctors there in the bunker,' I called as I saw the infantry carefully advancing down the slope, and then I followed my charges up the pathway.

Twenty paces had not been taken when shells from the defenders began falling in and around the village, which I later discovered was Fontaine-la-Mallet. There was a cry of "stretcher bearers" and leaving the tail of prisoners I rushed into the village to give help to the first aid men who were short handed. I helped carry one stretcher to the end of the rubble strewn road where my task was taken over by an ambulance crew.

I returned to the steep path and climbed to the top of the hill where the Bofors shells had so frightened our captors and where our carrier driver had made his escape.

Then I received a shock. Lying dead at the side of the path were three German soldiers. One wore highly polished jackboots and the uniform of an officer. It was unmistakably Captain Kurt Langner. His immaculate greatcoat that he had been so concerned to surrender in was torn and bloodstained and his peaked officer's cap lay alongside its owner's body. Next to him lay his faithful corporal. I hesitated. I stooped and picked up his cap. What a good souvenir to take back to my comrades! I turned away and pondered for a moment. No, I could not bring myself to take it. I felt genuinely sorry that he and his corporal were dead, killed accidentally by their own artillery. I put the cap back on to the ground and it rolled between the two men. No doubt someone else would take it in triumph and show around his unit as a legitimate keepsake. But I could not do that.

I continued forward. Where were Captain Thompson and Gunner Pearce? Which way had they gone? There were no other casualties that I could see. Eventually I came to a small group of soldiers where the path joined a road. Had they seen a party of prisoners? About forty of them? And two or three English soldiers with them, one a captain? They shrugged their shoulders and exhibited no interest. Some Jerries had been taken away in a truck, but they had not noticed any English soldiers with them. A feeling of rage came over me. The bloody Germans had been given a vehicle to take them to the rear and I who had captured them had been deprived of my companions and now had to walk who knew how far back to the guns. They might already be on the move without me!

It seemed a long walk back to the gun lines. I cannot recall any of the features. In fact I almost missed them and went trudging eastwards in to the unknown.

'Look who's here,' someone shouted. 'We thought you were dead.'

All my old mates crowded round and I did what I could to explain what had happened. It seemed that Captain Thompson had reported me missing, presumed dead. He had had another narrow escape from death for the shell that had killed the two Germans had fallen between them and Thompson but all the blast and shell splinters had gone in their direction so that he was merely bowled over.

George and Dennis fried some "liberated" potatoes as a celebratory meal. They tasted wonderful. Then I was packed off in George's jeep to the wagon lines to report to the second in command for de-briefing. He took one look at me and told me to have a good sleep first and that he would question me in the morning. I lay down in a farmyard with some blankets that were kindly lent to me and slept for twelve hours.

Le Havre fell the next day. British casualties had been light. From the 49th Division there had been nineteen killed and two hundred and eighty-two wounded. German casualties were much higher and were never accurately recorded. Eleven thousand two hundred prisoners had been taken. But the heaviest casualties had been amongst the civilians.

The dock area was so badly damaged by Allied bombing and enemy explosive charges that it was not operational for months. The other channel ports fell quite quickly, with the exception of Dunkirk which held out into 1945. But for some time the ports were unusable owing to the damage done to the docks and the mines that had been sewn in the harbour approaches. Because of this the High Command placed all their hopes on freeing Antwerp before sabotage could be carried out there. To that end British troops raced into Belgium and Holland, leaving the Canadians to take Dieppe, Boulogne and Calais. But for the 49th Division there was a period of rest. All units had been involved in almost continuous fighting since the landing at Arromanches and after the fierce but successful capture of Le Havre, the division was given three days rest. Bolbec was the nearest town and vehicles were organised to transport soldiers there every evening. The town had been undamaged and lights were shining in the houses and the town square. From the town hall came the sound of music where the town band was warming up for a dance in honour of the soldiers. Girls in their best dresses were gathered in groups giggling and ogling the visitors. The only drink that seemed to be available in the local estaminets was creme de menthe. Not exactly my favourite tipple. As the evening wore on the dance floor became crowded and emboldened by creme de menthe and other liquor that my party had not been able to locate, the hob-nail booted soldiery with sleeked down hair and grimy battledress became emboldened to seize the more forward of the local ladies. Balloons were blown up and patted around the room. Some flowed out into the square and down the street; delighted soldiers and their girls knocked them up into the air or burst them.

'Where on earth have they go the balloons from,' I asked in my innocence.

'They're not balloons — they're French letters.'

While on rest near Bolbec I had a strange experience. I was clearing out the carrier when Captain Thompson came up.

'We've got some visitors in the camp. You might have a good story to tell them.'

We walked across the green lines to where a group of khaki-clad men were standing conferring with notebooks in hand. They were dressed like officers but had no regimental markings or divisional markings. Two of them detached themselves from the group and came to meet us.

'You can say what you like to them,' said Captain Thompson. 'They are war correspondents searching for stories.'

'I hear that you've been taken prisoner and then escaped taking your captors captive,' asked one of the correspondents.

I nodded.

'Can you tell me your name and address?'

I looked at the man. I tried to say my name and address but nothing would come. 'Take your time. Just your name and address to start with.'

They stared at me, I looked away. Why couldn't I tell them such a simple thing? Why was I unexpectedly struck dumb like Zechariah in St Luke's Gospel?

'We'll come back in a few minutes,' said the war correspondent looking at me curiously. Did he think I was being difficult? Did he think I resented their appearance out of the blue and that I was being questioned about private matters that I did not want to divulge to the press? He walked away and spent some few minutes talking to other soldiers and making notes. Then he returned with a companion.

'We've got the story from your fellow-soldiers. All we want is your name and address.'

At last I spoke, 'I — I can't remember it, sir.'

They looked at me in disbelief.

'So you don't want to tell us.'

'No sir, I can't remember.' They walked away and left me. Captain Thompson and other soldiers eyed me strangely and then walked away too. I could not tell them who I was or where I lived. I did not want to be so reticent. I just could not get the words out.

I suppose I was suffering from some kind of delayed shock, what the medical profession would call a kind of hysteric reaction. But I felt very uneasy about myself and the way I had been seen to behave by others.

When it was time to move the colonel ordered a drive past so that he could inspect his regiment and take the salute. The column drove out of the meadows and up a gently winding road to the top of a hill where Charlie Handlebars stood.

He was able to look down and see all his regiment snaking up towards him. George Baker Able drove past, Lieutenant Cannell standing in the front at the salute. The colonel returned the salute and halted the vehicle.

'You've got too much gear aboard your vehicle. You look

The War memorial at Fountaine-la-Mallet, September 10th, 1989. Fountaine-la-Mallet was a German strong point in the defence of Le Havre, September 10-11th 1944. The village was awarded the Croix de Guerre.

like a dustcart. As soon as you are clear of this road dump all the extra rubbish.'

Lieutenant Cannell's face fell and he flushed. He was proud of his collection. Tied each side of the vehicle was a sheet of corrugated iron acquired to make a good, safe roof for his command post. On the roof was a large carpet rolled as neatly as possible. This was used to carpet the dug-out floor. Underneath swung a large frying pan and a metal bucket to be used for his ablutions. He drove on feeling robbed of legitimate protection . . . Lieutenant Cannell was disconsolate for days.

I observed this from my vantage point in the carrier OPA, for I was now part of Captain Thompson's observation crew and he did not want to lose the tried and tested team that had come through the ordeal of the assault on Le Havre.

7

The pursuit into Belgium and Holland

Once we had left Bolbec we made a rapid advance through Northern France gathering speed by the day. We halted in Lille and slept in a large hall. As we sped through villages and towns the people came into the street to greet us. The column was held up by cheering crowds. Pretty girls clambered on to the vehicles, thrust flowers into our hands, placed garlands around out necks and kissed us warmly. Men and women held out their hands to shake our hands and some climbed aboard in triumph. Bottles of wine were offered to us and we drank from the bottle, handing it round to our companions and to our welcomers. Often the mayor was there in his national sash and sometimes the town band would be playing to greet the liberators. There was cheering and laughter and tears.

'Vive les Anglais! Vive la France!'

'Vive Grand Bretagne! Vive nos amies!'

We moved into Belgium. The reception became even warmer. In one small town the column was brought to a halt for over an hour. Major Draper decided that we would spend the night there. We were invited into people's houses. We were offered wine and brandy and potato soup with bread. It was all delicious and exciting. Toast followed toast and our Flemish speaking hosts spoke of their Royal Family and we spoke of ours. It was a good job that the enemy was in full retreat since our thinly posted guards would have been easily overwhelmed by an attack.

It was strange to be advancing through territory that our fathers had fought over in World War I. Ypres, Poperinghe, Menin Gate were places that we passed through or passed by. Our fathers had fought the Hun and defeated him and now their sons were doing the same. It was a time of great elation. We were chasing the Boches, we were winning the war: soon we would be in Germany. What had seemed impossible in 1940 was being fulfilled in 1944. That invincible German war machine that had overrun most of Europe and brought with it a hideous occupation was now in headlong retreat. History was repeating itself and we were making the history!

As we moved further into Belgium the rapturous reception was shadowed by evidence of German rearguard action. At a crossroads there would be a knocked out vehicle, either British or German or both, and a sad roadside scene. A wooden cross or a rifle stuck muzzle down into the ground surmounted by a steel helmet. If it were British there would be a name scratched on to it or a piece of board with a name and number inscribed. If it were a German helmet that would be all. Beneath the helmet lay the body of some soldier killed a few hours before and hastily buried in a shallow grave. Each of these roadside scenes were evidence of some small but deadly encounter: a British tank knocked out by a hidden 88mm which in turn was knocked out by the following British tanks; an unsuspecting scout car rounding a sudden bend and being hit and set on fire by a determined soldier hidden in the ditch with a deadly Panzerfaust.

For some years after the war I used to have a bad dream about coming across a German ambush in the OPA carrier and being blown sky high! Sometimes when driving along a country lane I would visualise an enemy strong point at the next corner and see in my mind an ideal situation for an ambush. All imagination, but a reminder of the anticipation and stress imprinted deeply into my mind at an impressionable age.

As we drove along a straight stretch of road that seemed to go on forever into the flat Flemish landscape we saw a vast fleet of aircraft pass overhead. More followed to our left and then more again to our right.

'Blimey,' exclaimed the infantryman seated on the rear of the carrier with his companion, 'where are they going? I've never seen so many bleeding planes in all my life!'

I, too, had never seen so many aircraft in the air in formation before, and I had seen squadrons of Heinkels and Dorniers flying in formation over Kent to bomb the London Docks on September 7th 1940, and seen the American daylight bombers forming up over East Anglia in 1943. But this demonstration of air power was overwhelming.

'Look, there are gliders up there!'

Indeed there were. Many of the planes were towing gliders, two and even three at a time. The armada filled the skies for nearly ten minutes and the roar of the engines could be heard as an angry drone above the high noise of the carrier. We were to learn later that they were bound for Arnhem. We did not know of the fierce fighting that was to engulf them and how disastrous the enterprise, so high in expectation, was to be.

The carrier became low on petrol and I offered to replenish the tank from the Jerrycans strapped to the back of the vehicle. The carrier stopped and the engine was switched off, a very necessary precaution; the passengers leapt off, stretched their legs on the grass verge and proceeded to relieve themselves. I took off the petrol cap and using the canvas funnel supplied began to pour from the can. The weather was extremely warm. Riding in the carrier was like being cooked in a slow oven, except that our faces were exposed to the wind. Because of the intense heat the petrol vapourised and the metal frame being almost red hot caused the fumes to ignite and the petrol emerging from the can began to burn in a long steady flame. Hastily I closed the cap on the can and the flame went out, but there was petrol spilled on to the metal and there was imminent danger of the tank exploding because of the vapour at its mouth. The driver clambered up and pushed a blanket roll over the conflagration putting out the flames. We waited until the engine had cooled and then filled the tank with what petrol we had. We were all amazed at the heat and the way the petrol had vapourised and thought ourselves lucky once again that no disaster had occured.

We spent the night at what I believe was Aalst and then drove on skirting Brussels and heading north. The sign posts read Anver/Antwerpen to the left and Bruxelles/Brussel to the right. We were in the heartland of the Flemish speaking area, devoutly Roman Catholic and devoted to their Royal Family. Houses and farmsteads proudly displayed portraits of King Leopold and the Belgian flag hung in the trees and from window ledges. I remember thinking that if the British were being liberated there just would not be so many flags in people's homes to put on a comparable show.

One of the consequences of the long and dusty drives in such hot weather with the constant stream of air in the eyes was a form of conjunctivitis. I believed that I was the only one with stinging eyes. It seemed as if they were filled with grit. But it seemed that everyone who had travelled in open vehicles was suffering in the same way. When the column stopped there was a long queue for the medical officer who with his assistant proceeded to give us eye drops.

After several days of rapid movement the battery was deployed and prepared for action. I can recall spending a rather chilly night in a barn on radio watch. The wavelength was being jammed with interference. "Ziggly-diggly-ziggly-diggly" filled my ears through the earphones. I wondered if I could bear any more of this mental torture. Had I been required to send any messages through that mush of noise I doubt if anyone would have received even were they to be 200 yards away. In the morning the dispatch rider arrived with a new wavelength and call sign and we were back in business again.

'Hello all stations Peter Charlie, Report my signals.'

'Hello Peter Charlie 1, hello Peter Charlie 1, strength 4, over.'

The radio net began to build itself up.

Later that day Captain Thompson explained to his crew that the infantry company was to cross the Turnhout Canal by night and form a bridgehead so that the rest of the battalion could pass through and launch an attack against stiffening German resistance. It seemed from intelligence reports that the enemy was creating a line of defence based on the Canal. This was the first large scale opposition that we had met since taking Le Havre. When writing the narrative for this night action some forty-four years later I was lucky enough to come across a letter written to my mother soon after the event. Soldiers in this theatre of war were allowed to send letters in an envelope marked "Active Service Army Privilege Envelope". On the front of the envelope were a set of instructions which included this statement:

"I certify on my honour that the contents of this envelope refer to nothing but private and family affairs". This was then signed. As you will see when you read it I took a liberal view of what constituted private and family affairs, but I was always careful not to give times or places.

In a letter dated October 22nd I wrote:

> 'I think I may as well describe that incident when our brigade established a bridgehead over a canal. We had moved up quickly and went into action not far from the bank. We were the first troops in the area at the time, the infantry not having arrived yet. I was with the OP and we went to a village nearby for the night and to contact the Recce. Later we found that a big factory about half a mile away from the guns was full of Germans, the only thing being in between them and the guns was the cookhouse! Incidentally the White Brigade or Belgian Resistance, magnificently organised, cleared the enemy out of said factory the next day. That day at dusk our infantry with our carrier crossed over the canal and dug in in a semi-circle around the bridge. It was most eerie moving up into the hostile territory at walking speed, wondering what opposition we would meet. I had to have a blanket over my head and over the radio so as to muffle any noise when transmitting. We reached our objectives without any opposition and waited for the inevitable counter-attack. Obviously Jerry allowed us to cross the canal, so that he could counter-attack along the bank and cut us off. He nearly did it, too, at one time being only 100 yards from the bridge.
>
> Anyway, we settled down to uneasy sleep with some infantry in a big barn. At 3 am the Germans started to infiltrate into our positions under the cover of darkness.
>
> The forward section of our infantry became cut off, and dawn broke to find our position completely surrounded; the nearest enemy being 200 yards away in a hedge bottom. From 3 o'clock onwards I was sat in the carrier outside the barn manning the radio. Our position was

under small arms fire, and did those Spandau bullets zip and crackle over! It was a good job that the Germans did not have any mortars with them; as it was they did fire some rifle grenades at us. Two exploded in the roof about 20 feet from the carrier. I am no hero, but I could not resist peeping over the top of the carrier occasionally to see what was going on. The rest of the carrier crew were in the barn and our officer had to shout messages to me, as he could not reach me on account of enemy fire.

Our infantry were magnificent. They fired everything they had got, and we saw some of their work later when German prisoners came in. We had a machine gun mounted on our carrier salvaged from a tank and an infantry bloke was firing this straight ahead until the flaming thing jammed. Our captain decided to call our guns to help and we brought down a troop target on the Germans in the aforesaid hedge-bottom, It was what was called a "close target" because the enemy to be shelled were only 200 yards away from us. The designation of a "close target" meant that each gun-layer had to have his work checked by the gun position officer before the order to fire could be given. Our own shells exploded uncomfortably close and it pays tribute to our fire orders and the the gunners' accuracy that the rounds dropped fair and square on the target. Out of a dozen Germans, all were killed or wounded. Peeping over the side in the other direction I could see some bobbing heads and bottoms along a hedgerow some 70 yards away. They were German all right but I never found out where they went. They did not seem to fire at us.

I asked for some tanks (code named Big Boys) over the air and these came trundling up about an hour later, by which time the situation was less intense, thanks to our artillery support and the courage of our infantry. I saw a tank go right up to the window of a house about 400 yards away and open fire through the window with its gun. I pity the Germans inside. Altogether the infantry took 70 prisoners and I saw some horribly wounded casualties. I could not help feeling sorry for them. All the Germans were in bad shape being covered in mud and utterly fagged out.'

Reflecting upon that letter now brown with age, I can add one or two details. The German leader of the counter-attack was a middle-aged sergeant major. He wore the white piping of the infantry. I recall that when surrendering he kept looking at his wounded men and sadly shaking his head. The prisoners taken who were not casualties were ordered to dig graves for their men who had been killed. They were reluctant to do so fearing that they were digging their own graves. But this was not the intention. After the battle was over and the tanks had rumbled back carrying British and German wounded, an 88mm arrived upon the scene and proceeded to shell the bridge area. The Major's half-track was stationed just over the bridge and Bombardier Stead, the Major's gunnery assistant, was killed instantly by an exploding shell. I felt cut up about this for while he had never been a friend of mine he was a man I had always liked and respected. It seemed ironic that he should have been killed and not one of us at the forward OP where danger had been nearer. When we were relieved by fresh troops we re-crossed the canal and slept soundly after 24 hours of fear, sleeplessness and concentration.

A major problem faced by all the Allies in their advance was one of lengthened lines of communication. We were now 150 miles from the Normandy Beaches. All our petrol, ammunition and food had to be transported by truck from the Mulberry Harbour to wherever we found ourselves. The nearer we got to Germany the further our lines were stretched. This was why the enemy held on to the Channel ports as long as he could. So the advance, exciting and spectacular, began to peter out and the rounds per gun per day were severely rationed.

We ground to a halt having crossed the Turnhout Canal and were rested at a small town called Poppel. There was a steam tram service from there to Turnhout which became a popular place to visit.

A mobile bath unit was set up in a conveniently draughty field and half a troop at a time the men were driven there. It was well organised but the weather had turned cold. We wondered what the men who manned the bath unit would reply to their children after the war when asked, 'And what did you do in the army, Daddy?'

They seemed to be objects of some mirth at the time, but in all fairness in retrospect they performed an important function. As did our battery latrines digger, commonly know as the "shit house wallah."

At the baths George and I debated whether we would remain dirty but warm or become clean but cold. Somewhat reluctantly we allowed ourselves to be called into the bath unit. There were two large tents. In the first each soldier removed all his clothing except for his boots. His battledress was left to one side. He then had a shower which was reasonably warm so long as he was not in the last dozen by which time the water had run cold. He then emerged, replaced his boots, picked up his battledress and moved out into a wind-swept field before entering a second tent where clean socks, vest, shirt and underpants were piled for each man to collect for himself. In our nakedness plus ammunition boots I caught a glimpse of Maurice and we fell about laughing at the sight.

'By gum, Maurice, you look a fine figure of a man, you'll have all the girls around you.'

'Not bloody likely, I'm too frozen to be of any use to a girl. I feel like a snow-fruit.'

The great event of this short rest period was not the shower but going to the cinema.

The army had taken over the local cinema in Turnhout and was showing the latest Hollywood film "Going My Way", with Bing Crosby playing the part of a Catholic priest. Bing was a particular favourite of George, Dennis and myself and with our passes we climbed aboard the steam tram to drive to Turnhout some four miles away. The cinema was full of khaki clad figures wearing the insignia of the Polar Bear on their sleeves. Indeed the whole town was swarming with men of the 49th Division and we only just managed to get seats in the cinema. The lights in the auditorium went down accompanied by the whistles and cat calls of the audience. All went well until halfway through the film when it broke down in the middle of a a song. Instant hub-hub! After a few minutes of pandemonium the show recommenced but the picture and the sound were out of synchronisation. This was too much for George, ever the perfectionist in the field of performance.

'Come on, John,' he snorted, 'let's get out of here. I'd rather not see the film at all than have it ruined like this. Only the army could muck it up so effectively.'

Dutifully I followed and we walked around the town glowing with righteous anger until it was time to catch the tram back to the village where we were camped.

I recall that when we were in Turnhout a Belgian stopped us and said in excellent English, 'Excuse me, but may I make an observation. The thing we Belgians have noticed most about your soldiers is the way they deport themselves in the street. When the Germans were here (he called them Moffer which was the Dutch word for them) and we encountered them on the pavement we had to get out of the way always. We had to get off the pavement and into the road. But with your soldiers it is they who move out of the way and get into the road. This may seem trivial to you but to me it a mark of a civilised nation. Good day to you and God bless you.'

Our pleasant stay in the Turnhout area was soon to pass and we moved forward in deteriorating weather towards the Dutch border. I can recall several incidents at this time. The road bounded by trees had been heavily shelled by our guns and the tops of the trees had been badly shattered. We had caught a German patrol in the roadside and the shells exploding in and among the trees had killed many of them. As we waited for a move forward there was an almighty boom some little distance in front of us. There had been no warning whistle or whoop. It was not an explosive sound that we had heard before. We were mystified. Later we realised that it must have been a V2 rocket that had come down prematurely from a launching site somewhere in Holland. At that time the V2 was still a secret weapon, only the V1, the flying bomb, had been sent against England. The enemy had begun to launch the V1 soon after the Normandy invasion. The bombers had their launch sites in France, Belgium and Holland. One of the joys of the defeat of the German army in France was that the launching places of the V1's were cut off and over run. Our families and friends at home were being saved by our military exertions abroad. Unfortunately Holland was to prove too difficult to take that coming winter and the V2's continued

Round a 25-pounder.
Right, Tiffy Newson, Left, Sgt Davis, Centre, L/Sgt. Scott.

to rain on London and the South-East almost to the very end of the war.

On one other occasion Lieutenant Mitchell, a huge, gentle young man with very light blue eyes, a great rugby player and popular with the men, was acting forward as troop commander. He had driven into the courtyard of a large farmhouse and halted. He and his carrier crew waited for other officers to arrive before holding a conference about the next move. As they gathered round a map spread on the bonnet of one of the trucks a previously hidden German opened up on the assembled men with a machine gun. Several fell wounded. Mitchell himself was skimmed by a bullet that entered his helmet and took out the nut holding the headpiece together. There was an immediate reaction to this unexpected attack. The surprised soldiers grabbed their weapons and made for the barn firing as they went. The sound of small arms fire rattled and crackled all around the farm. After a few moments of confusion two dead Germans were dragged out followed by a handful of terrified live ones hands above heads and shaking like leaves. They were stood against the wall and would have been shot out of hand had not one of the senior officers ordered a cease fire. It seemed that of the hidden men only one had wanted to continue the fight and he had silenced the others on pain of death. So one fanatic had sold his life dear for the sake of the Fatherland and taken another with him for the score of several British officers wounded.

It taught us yet another lesson. Be sure to clear all the barns and other buildings before relaxing guard. A determined enemy would be prepared to lie low for hours if need be.

As we approached the Dutch border the brigade was held up by gun and mortar fire. The intensity of this we had not met since the days in the bocage.

The enemy had good observation over the flat terrain and every movement was spotted. It became clear that the OP was in the tall church tower in the large village of Hoogstraten. Our carrier was forward with a company of the South Wales Borderers led by a young, voluble Welsh officer who had not been long out from Britain. His men were held up by the enemy shelling and Spandau fire and they took up defensive positions in a wood surrounded by stone walling, on the edge of the village.

Charlie Handlebars arrived in his jeep to assess the situation.

'We can't advance against such a strong position under observation.' The discussion with the infantry leaders went on.

'This place reminds me of that comedian on the wireless, Gillie Potter. He says he is talking to England from Hogsnorton — that's like the name of this place, isn't it? I shall call it Hogsnorton from now on!'

The 25-pounders were ordered to fire at the spire of the church tower. The colonel watched with his field glasses.

'It's no good, we're missing the tower. Call up an anti-tank gun, one of the big 17-pounders.'

The anti-tank gun duly arrived and was laid carefully on the target. Several armour piercing shells were fired. There was one hit which chipped some of the masonry.

'That's no good either. We'll be here all day trying to knock Jerry out of the tower like that. We need something more powerful. Call up the Typhoons!'

After a while, contact with the airforce was made through the elaborate radio network. At the right time the guns fired red smoke at the base of the tower to indicate the target to the fast flying aircraft. As the smoke drifted away a typhoon fighter-bomber screamed in over our position and fired its rockets slung under its wings. The noise was alarming. We were some 800 yards from the church but it seemed as if the rockets were intended for us. There was a series of orange and red flashes and a pall of dense black smoke rose from around the tower. A second Typhoon screamed into the attack and the tower erupted in flame and smoke.

Silence followed. The top of the tower was missing. The infantry moved forward through the wood and began to enter the village. By nightfall the village was clear and all opposition had ceased.

At last we crossed into Holland. The terrain became even flatter and was criss-crossed with drainage ditches. The weather began to deteriorate rapidly. Cold rain was followed by frost at night. Our objective was to take the town of Rosendaal and proceed to clear the enemy out of North-West Brabant as far as we could. As we deployed in a wet landscape George, Dennis and I designed our masterpiece of a dug out. We could not dig down more than a couple of feet because of the water table. We dug three trenches in the drizzling rain in the shape of a star. Where the trenches came together we extended the hole and built a fire place out of long ammunition boxes. The trenches were covered with shell boxes filled with earth and our bedding was laid on top of the ground sheets, one to a trench. Each one of us slid in feet first so that our heads met by the fire and there was room to roll over on to our stomachs and attend to the cooking. Thus we had good protection, could talk to each other and generally feel warm and domesticated. Turning out in the middle of a wet night became an unpleasant prospect, however.

Others were called over to admire our desirable accommodation. The fireplace burning cordite bags and damp sticks really impressed them.

'How much do you charge for bed and breakfast?'

'What are you going to call your palace — the Ritz?'

We stood back and admired our handiwork. There was nothing to be said to the coveteous but go and do likewise!

In the night and through the morning the guns took part in a barrage preparatory to assaulting Rosendaal. Over to the right the tanks of the Polish Armoured Division rumbled forward to support our infantry. The town was ablaze with a pall of smoke hanging over it. Then the attack was halted. We stayed in our damp field for a few days and then we were ordered forward avoiding the town. It was clear that we had a damp and cold time ahead of us. As Jim was to say on several occasions during the next month.

'Winter campaign, George?'

'Yes, Jim, winter campaign.'

'Winter campaign, John?'

'Yes, Jim, winter campaign.'

When we had been back in Normandy in the Demouville area we had been visited by an army padre. He had dropped down into our mosquito infested dug out and asked if we would like to be confirmed. He would prepare us for confirmation. After some hesitation George and I had agreed to put ourselves forward. We were not church-goers but it seemed a kind of insurance in the time of battle and in any case we felt that we liked the padre. No more was seen of him and we heard no more until one day in late October he turned up on the gun site and informed us that the service would be taken by the Bishop of Dover in two days time in newly liberated Eindhoven.

'I'm sorry I haven't been able to give you any instruction at all, but I've had other things to do and it's been quite impossible to keep trace of all units since the break out. But you'll be all right, won't you?'

We said that we supposed that we would be.

'You'll go up to the front and the Bishop will lay his hands on your head and you will affirm your faith in Christ. It's quite simple to follow the service.'

So on the appointed day we climbed aboard a 3-tonner and drove around many army positions picking up a soldier here and a soldier there. The truck drove us to the large car park belonging to Philips Electrics. Once on the tarmac we were directed to the theatre belonging to the firm. Philips had a good record in looking after their workers in the 1930s.

In the theatre were several hundred men. Goodness only

knows how many regiments were represented and how the organisation to get them all there had been carried out.

The Bishop of Dover arrived and conducted the service. I was impressed at the time by his sermon but cannot for the life of me remember anything of it now. Then it was the time for the laying on of hands. To my surprise I saw Gunner Medhurst going forward. He knelt before the Bishop. Medhurst was the last person I had expected to see there. He was one of the gun numbers in "A" Troop, a big, tough looking man with a crewcut. But I remembered that he was a gentle person and I had never seen him in any kind of scrape. George and I came away from the service somewhat awed and subdued, not quite sure what we had done nor what we had had done to us. But the picture of Medhurst and all those other soldiers of all ranks and regiments dressed in mud-stained battledress and wearing ill-polished boots, kneeling before the Bishop, stayed in my mind for a long time — and still returns from time to time.

Our gun position was now situated in the village of Oudgastel. There was not a lot of activity. The Germans had withdrawn to the other side of Holland Diep, part of the mouth of the Scheldt. We could not advance beyond the flooded land around Stampersgat. As the enemy retreated the gates of the sluices were opened and large areas were flooded. I remember standing with Wally Coldrick, another signaller, with some Dutch boys playing in a back garden. I seem to remember being concerned about them lest they got into any kind of danger. There were always cartridge cases lying around and guns with ammunition. Suppose the enemy opened fire unexpectedly and killed some of the children? I cannot recall much of this period. We camped out in barns and outhouses and cow byres. We met for the first time the small Dutch farmer whose cow shed led straight into his kitchen. The smell of the cows, sweet and pungent permeated the whole of the cottage. All rooms were scrupulously clean, including the cow byre, but we never got used to the smell. Sometimes we slept over the cows in the straw loft above and were lulled to sleep by the munching of the cows chewing the cud. Sometimes we were invited to sleep in the kitchen. Sometimes were were offered a bed.

Above, Stempersgat, near Maas. Flooded by the Germans. October/November, 1944.

Below, Our gun position at Oiedgastel. Walley Coldwich and the author, November, 1944.

This we usually refused feeling too dirty to sleep in a real bedroom on a real bed.

In early November the division moved to the east and were involved in fighting around Weert, crossing the Wessem Canal, and moving towards the border town of Venlo on the Maas and close to Germany.

I was by this time no longer a member of the carrier crew having rejoined the guns in GBA.

There is only one incident of this period that stands out in my mind. Just before an attack we carried out a night occupation. We had been told that there was a German self-propelled gun lurking around in the neighbourhood. Moving guns at night is always a tricky exercise. They have to be unlimbered, quads driven away, aiming post set up and guns aligned accurately — all in darkness and with minimum noise. A night picket was used for the guns to aim their sights on to. This was a battery operated red light that had to be fixed where all gun layers could see it. I volunteered to place the night picket on top of a hen house and tie it up there with string. So I climbed up on to the sloping roof of the hen house with some trepidation scaring numerous chickens as I did so. They ran off squawking in all directions and making enough noise to alert anyone within a mile. As I clung to the roof tying the light into place with string, the enemy self-propelled gun began to shell the field. The firing was very accurate, the shells landing in and around our guns and vehicles. We were caught in the open before there had been any chance to dig in.

I descended from my hen roof much quicker than I had ascended.

Bringing a section of it with me I hit the ground with a bump and lay as flat as I could. About a dozen shells came over. We could hear the gun fire, hear the whistle of the approaching shells and prepare ourselves for the explosion. It was not an 88mm but a less high velocity gun, probably a 75mm.

Everyone flung himself to the ground, hugging Mother Earth as tightly as possible. There were vivid flashes and lumps of earth and stones were flung in the air showering some of the lads with debris. We braced ourselves for further explosions as we heard the gun fire again and again. The shells arrived with their whistle and there was a series of dull plops. They were duds and failed to explode. But the last to arrive went off with an almighty crack. Only the first and the last were effective!

No one was hurt.

'Thank God for the slave workers,' cried Fred Dalton, 'they've filled the shells with sawdust to sabotage the Nazi war effort!'

The night picket was straightened up and the guns aligned and the troop was ready for action.

"MIKE TARGET! MIKE TARGET! MIKE TARGET!

The OP was determined to catch that German gun. A Mike Target of four rounds gunfire was ordered and carried out. We did not know if we had hit our enemy before he could move away from his assumed position, but we did not hear from him any more.

One day as we were digging in and George was planning an even more ambitious dug out (for we were now on higher ground and could therefore dig deeper once more), a buzz went round the gun position.

'Tedder's boys are up.' remarked Jim, observing the fighter/bombers of the Tactical Air Force going over us to strafe the enemy.

'Yes, Jim, Tedder's boys are up. Winter Campaign, eh?'

'Yes, John, Winter Campaign.'

'Have you heard the latest?' said one of the other signallers, hot foot from the command post where Lieutenant Cannell was supervising his latest improvement in protection after several weeks of unsatisfactory cow byres and outhouses.

'We're coming out on rest!'

'On rest? Where to?'

It turned out that we were to be completely withdrawn from the line and return to Belgium. Our destination was Roeselare not far from the French border. We drove in convoy, glad to be away from the mud and the dangers. We slept in or under the vehicles just as we had done on our first night ashore in Normandy. As then there was anti-aircraft fire as shells were fired into the star-filled sky but this time at V1 Flying Bombs passing overhead.

We halted at a place called Erps-Kwerps, just outside Brussels. What a strange name I thought. By this time I was feeling ill. I had a fever and stomach ache. I emptied my bowels whenever we stopped. The most inconvenient place was outside someone's wood shed in the middle of the night with the crackling of shell bursts overhead. Erps-Kwerps seemed a fitting name!

We reached Roeselare early in the morning and stood by our vehicles. An advance party had worked out civilian billets for everyone. I was sent to a cottage in a row in the centre of the town. It was occupied by two elderly Flemings, Pauline and Joseph Breskels. I was shown into a white, simply furnished room with a feather bed and clean white sheets and blankets. I washed as best as I could and climbed into bed. The chamber pot remained a very real necessity. The following morning I went to the window and looked out. Men of our battery were moving about below ready to have roll call.

'Bill, tell the Sergeant-major that I'm not well and I intend to stay in bed here at No 46 for a couple of days until I am fit.'

In normal military circumstances such a message on my part would have been unthinkable, but such was the trust and comradeship that had been built up in the troop during the campaign that such an unorthodox communication was accepted. A few minutes later the Sergeant-major came to the foot of the cottage and called up to me.

'Mercer, you should report sick, but just this once you can stay where you are. I'll come and see how you are tomorrow.'

After twenty-four hours I had slept and sweated my fever away. Whether I had just caught a chill or whether I had a mild form of dysentery I never knew. What was remarkable was that I had kept well through five months of heat, rain, frost and wind living rough and in the open most of the time. The idea of living rough today fills me with alarm. But I was younger then. I was so lucky not to have had even a cold in the head until this time when I could actually go to a real bed and sweat myself better in nature's way.

Old Pauline and her husband looked after me like a

mother and father, emptying the pot and bringing me warm soup and brandy. They were most appreciative of the army ration that we brought them. Of all the items they best liked the tablets of soap.

'You don't smell like the German soldiers,' they said.

'How did they smell?' I queried.

'It is not easy to say. But their soap was not good. And we had to use it too. It was ersatz.'

That was the smell that we were to meet again when occupying quarters that the enemy had just vacated, and that we were to smell in German civilian houses too.

The Belgians had plenty of potatoes and a little pork. I was amazed at the tasty meals that Pauline could produce with potatoes and vinegar and a little margarine or oil.

One day Joseph said that there was a local small-holder who wanted to entertain some English soldiers to thank them for freeing his country from the occupying Germans. George, Dennis and I got ready and in the early afternoon the man arrived with his donkey cart. We clambered aboard and set off out of town along a poplar lined road that got progressively narrower. After about two miles the cart turned off the road down a farm track until it arrived at the small-holding. We were bidden to enter and were introduced to his wife and young children. We gave them gifts of chocolate and soap. A meal of pork and potatoes was ready for us. It was clear that a pig had been specially slaughtered for the occasion. We smiled and nodded and drank several toasts. We caught the eye of old Joseph and he smiled back at us and winked. The farmer and his family were not very clean and the farmhouse smelt of pigs and dirty washing and unwashed human beings. I had a job to eat up my generous helping of pork and had to force myself out of politeness to smile and say how good it was. Further helpings were offered but refused. We felt awkward and were glad when we were able to make our excuses and leave. The farmer was clearly disappointed that we were not able to eat more and to drink a second bottle of his brandy.

'Phew,' we said, 'didn't that place smell awful?'

Joseph nodded and smiled. In our broken French we exchanged confidences. The farmer had been kind to Joseph and Pauline during the occupation giving them black market rations. He was a rough man but had a heart of gold. It was his way of thanking us for the liberation of Belgium. As a pig farmer in that part of Flanders at that time he knew no better.

George and his family used to visit Ostend and stay there on holiday before the war. George's parents used to take their six children to stay at the Hotel Ibis whose proprietor was a Mr Nassens. George was determined to try to find the hotel and its friendly owner. Although Ostend was some thirty miles from Roeselare it would not be too difficult to get there by motor bike. He managed to borrow an ancient bike owned by a relative of Pauline. The petrol he scrounged from one or two of our trucks, a little here a little there and persuaded me to accompany him on pillion. We found our way there easily enough. However finding the Hotel Ibis proved more difficult. In fact we never did find it. The beach and promenade were sealed off with barbed wire, minefields and pill boxes. There were numerous signs declaring 'ACHTUNG MINEN' bearing the outline of the skull and crossbones. The Germans were nothing if not dramatic. The side roads to the beach were clogged with abandoned vehicles, accumulated rubbish and sand. None of the people we came across as we drove around seemed to know where the hotel was or had been. Most of them were strangers to the town being refugees from other parts of Belgium. The centre of the town where the shops and bazaars were located was dead. George found it difficult to accept that he could not find the place and could not find anyone who had even heard of Mr Nassens.

'It's only six years ago that we were last here. It's all wrong, John. The place has so changed. It's terrible. I wish I had never come.'

As it was getting dark I suggested that we should be heading back to Roeselare before we got ourselves lost in some unperceived minefield. Slowly and with many stops we got back to Roeselare. I was very stiff and cold, but relieved to return safely to my billet and comfortable bed. We had not been missed. Then the unexpected and upsetting happened.

The colonel called us all together, battery by battery. We

assembled in a field and then were ordered to form a square around him. He told us that he had been awarded the OBE but this was an honour that really belonged to each one of us since it was an award given on the strength of his regiment. He was merely the figurehead, we were the body that made it all possible.

In a voice charged with emotion he went on to say.

'I have sad news for you. This regiment of which I am so proud to command is to be disbanded. I have protested in the strongest manner that is available to me, but all to no avail. You will in the course of the next week be sent to other units. I hope that you will all be able to remain in the Royal Artillery to which you belong and have so well distinguished yourselves. I wish you all God speed and good luck. Dismiss the parade, Major Draper.'

If Charlie Handlebars felt upset we were shattered. Be posted to other units! Have our tight comradeship split up! After all we had been through! But the worst was yet to come. Several days later we were told that only army tradesmen were to be kept in the artillery. Gunners and drivers were to be re-mustered and sent to infantry units. Bloody hell! George and Dennis and I were to remain in the artillery. Gun artificers and driver/ operators were classed as tradesmen. But what of our mates who were gun numbers and drivers?

A feeling of dread came over everyone in our regiment. This feeling was compounded by dismay at the break up of the warm comradeship and pride in the mob that had been forged over a long period and tested in battle since June. To many of the regiment the comradeship went back to before the war when they had joined as Territorials in the West Riding of Yorkshire. These had spent some time in Iceland when they were sent to hold that island against the possibility of invasion in the dark days of 1940. That was why the Division was called the Polar Bears and had a defiant polar bear as its emblem.

There was also a cold fear felt by many of those going into the infantry. We all knew it was the poor bloody infantry that bore the brunt of battle and suffered the highest casualties. How would our gunners fare with the minimal infantry training that they were likely to be given?

As the days went by the lads destined for the infantry were driven away. We watched our pal Smudger Smith wave forlornly from the back of the 3-tonner as it drove away. His face was a picture of misery. The guns and carriers were parked and covered over. The regimental trucks were taken over by other units. It was like the slow death of a living person. Finally only the tradesmen and the maintenance staff were remaining. The tradesmen were destined to go to Bourg Leopold, the former Belgian Army centre, between Brussels and Louvain. On December 23rd we said farewell and thanks to our civilian hosts. Pauline hugged me hard and tears ran down her cheeks. Joseph shook me by the hand and then clasped me to his chest. He too was crying. As we went to board our transport (3-tonners no longer belonging to us) George in a cold fury pushed his Sten gun down a drain and tossed the magazines after it. We all had our full service marching order on and as one who had ridden in a jeep for so long he was not prepared to carry any excess.

'I've never fired this thing and I don't suppose I ever will.'

I wondered if I should follow suit as part of the suppressed protest about our dismemberment. But I hesitated. After all I was rather proud of my German rifle acquired at Le Havre.

Bourg Leopold proved to be a vast, soulless cantonment. The Belgian version of Catterick. Naked light bulbs hung from the ceiling. Half of them were not working. We threw our equipment down on wire beds. No one asked about the whereabouts of George's small arms. My Mauser was taken away from me with a rebuke from the orderly corporal.

'What's this? You can't have a German weapon in the British army. Report to the CO tomorrow at 0900 hours.'

So much for natural justice! But the next morning was Christmas Eve and all was forgotten. I turned up later at my new unit and was promptly issued with a rifle!

To our delight passes were issued for us to go into Brussels for Christmas Eve. We had to report back at 9 am on Christmas morning. I cannot remember much about that Christmas Eve. Lights were on dimly in the cafes and shops. I think there was an attempt to illuminate Manniken Pis in

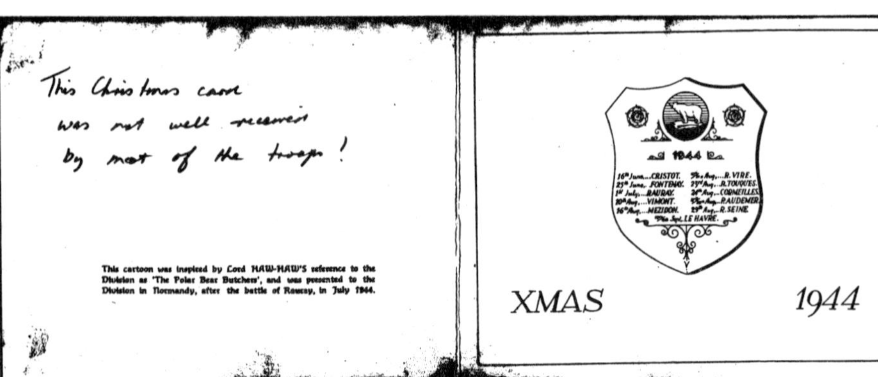

The 'Butcher Bear is seen standing at his chopping block at the sign-post to RAURAY. He is dressed in his blue & white apron and has his 'steel' slung round his waist. He is snarling and a few drops of blood drip from his great jaws. His right paw is toppling over a Panther. His left paw is poised over a butchers knife stuck in the belly of an SS bastard. More SS bastards each with a gory belly wound, lie beside him left. Around him brewed up Panthers & Mk IV specials and one Tiger; each show their swastikas. A few bodies lie around the brewed up Bosch tanks. There is a background of 'bocage' through which can be seen the muzzles of British 75's & 17 pdrs, also a Bren or two, all firing. Above the bocage two conventional flagstaffs fly the burgees of the —— 24 Lancers & Tyneside Scots.

PRINTED BY BREPOLS

This Christmas Card was not well received by most of our fighting troops.

Above, the outside, below the inside pages

one of the squares. Four or five of us wandered from cafe to cafe meeting up with others that we knew from time to time. There was a good deal of forced jollity. Many civilians abroad in the streets wished us a happy Christmas. Overhead all night long the V1 doodle-bugs rumbled and roared on their way to London. I did not drink enough to get drunk, merely to get very sleepy.

Around 3 o'clock in the morning I persuaded George to call it a day and we picked up a military vehicle that took us back to the camp. We turned in for a few hours sleep. At 9 am we were wakened by the officers and warrant officers bringing around tea and rum. This is an old British army tradition. Tea and rum in bed for the other ranks on Christmas morning. This was followed by Christmas dinner served by the officers once more. This cheered us all up a little. But the traditional fare and the incongruous surroundings coupled with the drink of the night before had a depressing effect on me. I thought of home and family and for the first time since landing in Normandy I felt really miserable. I lay on my hard mattress and fell into an uneasy sleep.

On Boxing Day George had great plans. He had seen on a poster in Brussels on the eve of Christmas that there was to be a classical concert at the Palais de Beaux Arts in the Belgian capital. We were to get to it by hook or by crook. He reported to the duty officer who rather grudgingly gave passes for him and me to be absent until 5 pm on that day. We left the camp, hailed a tram and arrived at the Palais just as the concert was beginning by playing the national anthems of Belgium and Great Britain. The luxuriously appointed auditorium was filled with well dressed Belgians. We must have been the only two English soldiers in the place. We got to our seats apologetically and sat down to enjoy the programme. It was a revelation to me since it was my first symphony concert. I cannot recall the name of the orchestra nor the conductor but it was entrancing to see the members of the orchestra at work: the conductor with his baton, the violins moving in unison, the brass coming in at exactly the right note, the woodwinds adding their counter melody and the percussion, so dominant and exciting. I can, however, remember two of the works played, Beethoven's 5th and Dvorak's New World. Both firm favourites of George who had them on records at home. To me these popular classics were the beginning of a love of symphonies. It is strange to think that had it not been for the army I might never have had this introduction to music, nor George my mentor. I have far more to owe to George than this introduction for nine years later I was to marry his sister, Joan.

On December 27th we knew our fate. George was to be posted to the 5th Regiment of the Royal Horse Artillery, equipped with self-propelled guns. Maurice was posted to a regiment in the 52nd Lowland Division. But Dennis and I were to remain together being sent to a newly formed unit, the Counter Mortar Officer's Staff of the 7th Armoured Division. So although George was to be in another unit we were at least in the same division, the 7th Armoured of North African fame.

8

A new mob and into the Third Reich

Dennis and I arrived in the Dutch coal mining town of Sittard in Limburg Province after Christmas. Snow had fallen quite heavily and the frost held throughout the day. Sittard was undamaged by the war and had some picturesque old houses as well as modern miners' houses outside the medieval town. We were lodged in a clean, modern house of a miner's family who received us quietly and without fuss. From the window of my room I could see cooling towers and slag heaps which were illuminated by floodlighting even though the war zone was only a few miles away. It seemed as if the Dutch in this part of Holland at least believed the war to be almost over and wanted to get back to normal as quickly as possible. One of the first things that we did was to go to the mine and enter the pit-head baths. This was altogether a more pleasant experience than we had had in the open field bath unit. The showers were hot and we could soap ourselves over and over again. We kept our own clothes and were warm all the time. It seemed to be a very modern mine, and I recall some of the other soldiers who had been miners back home saying how much better the conditions were in the mines in Holland. In fact much of what we saw in Europe in 1944 and 1945 seemed better than we were used to at home. All the houses had double glazing and none of the plumbing appeared to be on the outside of the houses inviting disaster when there was icy weather.

The Division put on a pantomime helped by some visiting artists from ENSA. I recall we saw a Sergeant Terry Thomas, he of the gap-tooth, who was later to make his name in a big way in the field of entertainment.

The latest popular song was "Long ago and far away" from a film starring the luscious Rita Hayworth. This song featured prominently in the programme. I have only the haziest recollection of the production but I have a mental picture of cigarette smoke, conviviality, nostalgia and temporary oblivion to the war.

The new unit, the Counter Mortar Officer's Staff (CMOS), was in the process of expansion. It had no guns and a rather unusual role. There were two OP's each carried in a half-track with radio communication to each other and to a headquarters section. The task of the CMOS was to push the OP's forward as far as possible. They were to listen for the sound of enemy mortars, to get a cross bearing and send the information back instantly to the HQ section which would send a map reference to the Commander Royal Artillery (CRA) who would speedily order a Mike Target with the guns. The idea was to catch the enemy mortars, which had caused so much damage in Normandy, before they could up sticks and move to another position.

The 7th Armoured Division, the Desert Rats, had had a distinguished war record in North Africa and Italy. It had been withdrawn from the Italian Campaign in order to retrain for the Normandy Invasion. Its experience in the bocage had been difficult. Some observers believed that its members were still thinking in military terms of the Western Desert and were not able to adjust to the new campaign conditions. Others thought that the division had been too long in battle and its soldiers were war weary. It seemed to us coming from the 49th Division that some of the Desert Rats were "bomb happy" and not always predictable in behaviour either in battle or off duty. But I must be careful not to malign a Division that had and still was making history. Few people back home had heard of the Polar Bears whereas everyone knew of the Desert Rats.

When we moved out of Sittard our OP took up a position in the small village of Holtum in a convent overlooking fields and ditches beyond which lay the enemy based on the town of Susteren. The observation post was established in the roomy loft of the convent from where we had a view across the frozen and sometimes fog bound fields. A skylight was opened to give us freedom of observation but it also allowed in the bitter cold. To our delight we were issued with newly designed tank suits which were warm and heavy being lined with kapok and made out of some kind of light canvas. They had elasticated wrists and ankles to keep out the cold. In fact they were an early and clumsy version of the track suit. We felt very privileged to have them and they made the cold nights on watch much more bearable. The smell of apples stored in the loft permeated the atmosphere. Whenever I smell apples in storage my mind goes back to that loft in Holtum. The good nuns left us severely alone. After all a group of licentious soldiery was an unattractive invasion of their privacy. They were, however, discreetly sympathetic. It seems that they had hidden Dutchmen and escaped Allied airmen on the run during the occupation by many subterfuges.

One young Dutchman, who seemed to be living under the protection of the sisters, spent a good deal of time with our crew talking, mainly about sex. He was hoping to learn from the British soldiers and was told so many tales that his sex life must have been subject to some very strange impulses. Our OP commander was not an officer but a sergeant, Sergeant Lloyd. There was a bombardier driver, a cook, a gunner observer and the two signallers, Dennis and myself.

It was while we were at Holtum that the Ardennes offensive by the German army took place. This massive last attempt to split the Allied armies and reach the sea was launched in the American sector to our east through the Ardennes forests. The brunt of the attack was taken by the Americans at a time when heavy cloud prevented the use of the allied air supremacy and when the snowy conditions favoured the surprise attack.

Many units of the British army were diverted to aid the Americans but our division was unaffected and continued to hold the position opposite the Roer River.

Night after night I would stare out from the loft across the frozen fields and listen for the sound of enemy mortars. They were rare indeed. The action was elsewhere. But I did hear night after night the sound of a motorcycle, the rumble of a tank, the noise of vehicles being driven along. These sounds followed the same pattern and were repeated at regular intervals. I reported that I suspected an amplified recording was being played across the battle zone in order to give us false evidence of enemy activity. This report was subsequently confirmed.

The frost turned to fog. Dense swirls of cold fog came across from the direction of Susteren. We peered into the fog half expecting enemy tanks followed by infantry to appear in the street below us. Then the Division went over to the offensive. An attack on Susteren was mounted. The intention was to clear all German forces out of the Roer pocket.

It was strange to listen to the artillery bombardment and see the barrage light up the sky when we ourselves were not responsible for the fire orders. No longer were we bringing down Mike Targets! Dennis and I felt we had become rather marginal.

We left Holtum and travelled by night along the single road to Susteren. There had been a temporary thaw and there was mud everywhere. Progress was slow. The enemy were putting up a stiff resistance. As well as the "pop-pop-brup" of Spandaus and the rattle of Bren guns there was the crump of enemy shell fire unpleasantly close and the occasional burst of mortar bomb. We would soon be in business after all!

We came to a bridge over a narrow river on the edge of the town where the scene was illuminated by blazing houses and barns. A field ambulance had been hit by enemy shell fire and was ablaze. Figures ran to and fro in the confusion trying to put out the flames and to move it off the bridge as it was successfully blocking access to the town. Infantry of the Queen's ran over the bridge to storm a German machine gun post, slipping and sliding in the mud as they took cover by the riverbank. It was a scene reminiscent of Dante's Inferno — all fire and smoke and cries of pain and anger. After what seemed like an hour during which some of us in the half-track got out and helped to push the ambulance over the bridge and out of harm's way, the bridge was clear and the fire in the ambulance extinguished. In fact only a few minutes had elapsed.

Many years later I was to discover that my future brother-in-law was one of the ambulance crew. Fate had decreed that we should pass each other on the Susteren bridge in the fiery night, and only find out how our paths had crossed in casual conversation years later.

The rest of the night was spent in the cellar of a house in the main street. It had been occupied by the enemy and only abandoned under the hour. The cellar was still warm and smelt of that ersatz soap that Pauline had spoken about. There was no concern for lice and typhus this time. We were only too glad to lie down on the mattresses and get some rest. Once more there were difficulties in maintaining the radio net. All night long as I remained on listening watch I heard the voice of a German operator somewhere near at hand calling 'Marco, Marco'. We had crossed wavelengths. His melancholy, high pitched voice went on and on calling 'Marco, Marco'. I never knew whether he ever made the contact that he was seeking but he effectively stopped us from communicating with our other units. He sounded so forlorn and desperate — almost like a persistent ghost voice.

Susteren was cleared by the infantry of the Queen's, and our OP moved forward and occupied a farm looking across moorland towards the village of Montfort. There we had an interesting experience. An artillery OP of the American army moved in with us and we shared observation, rations and comradeship. The Americans lived on KP rations which were good but had no fresh food. We, on the other hand, had a more limited menu, but had fresh meat, vegetables and bread sent up to us. We were delighted with KP tinned butter. They were delighted with Irish stew, straight from the pot, for we had our own cook. We noted one or two things about the American soldiers. No doubt they did so about us. One impression was that the Americans were more aggressive and argumentative towards each other. Another was that they did not give their officers so much respect as we did ours.

The British class and educational system did produce a division between officers and other ranks. There was diffidence and respect even when a particular officer was less than efficient.

With the Americans there was some resentment between the enlisted men and the officers. "Jack's as good as his master" as the old adage goes. The British class system had and has many shortcomings but it did produce a clear definition of leadership and deference to those in authority.

We also noticed an antipathy by some of the Americans towards a soldier of Red Indian extraction. In those days a black or Asian soldier in the ordinary units of the British Army was extremely rare and we prided ourselves on racial tolerance, probably quite falsely. The days of Commonwealth immigration were yet to come. After several days the Americans moved out and our advance towards the Roer continued. Our half-track entered the village of Montfort at dusk just behind the infantry. There had been a skirmish around the village street and a German soldier lay dead but still warm in the middle of the road. As we moved ourselves into the cover of a house I grabbed Les, the driver, by the arm.

'Les, I want a belt off that dead soldier.' Dennis Bold heard my remark and tried to stop me.

'How can you do that to a dead body? Leave him alone. He's some mother's son.'

Seized by a desire for a German leather belt I was not put off.

'He's dead. He doesn't need that belt anymore. I do. I won't be doing him any harm.' Squeamish I had been over taking Hauptman Langner's peaked cap. I no longer felt squeamish. Had I been hardened by experience?

Les helped me lift the body and I removed the belt and held it up in triumph. It was a good one, newly issued, with a splendid buckle "Got mit uns". I put it round my waist. It fitted exactly. I do not write this down with any pleasure. It does not portray me in a favourable light. I look back upon this incident and wish I had not done it. I did not keep the belt for very long. I cannot remember just what happened to it, but I suspect it was abandoned when I joined the 3rd Regiment Royal Horse Artillery in the Autumn of 1945.

Our final stop was in Posterholt. There were some empty houses, quite new, a contrast to most of the older buildings. They were on a small housing estate built for prosperous

Dutchmen. Eagerly we took possession for the weather was extremely cold again. We had petrol burning pressure stoves for our cooking and that was done in the open in case of fire. Bill Mountfort, our cook, got cracking and we had a large container full of hot tea. By the time some of the lads had got their mugs from the half-track, the tea was luke warm, cold in ten minutes and frozen in fifteen. We were amazed at how cold it must have been.

During our short stay in that village there were two incidents of a lighter vein. News came that other ranks could now wear collars and ties and also shoes. Before that only officers could dress in that way.

Dennis, being in the tailoring trade, set about altering shirts. He took cuffs to make collars and strips of shirting to make ties. We all carried needle and thread and spare buttons in our packs. He made a tie for me and converted one of my shirts to have a collar. He did the same for himself and offered to do the same for any other member of the OP. He was kept busy for two days, sitting cross legged on the floor of the house busily cutting and sewing. Most of the lads were delighted to donate a spare shirt for the enterprise and were pleased that our tiny unit was able to out-smart many of the others who would have to wait for official issue. Shoes were another matter. These could not be so easily manufactured. We knew we would have to wait until we should come across some in an abandoned house somewhere. That would not be looting we told ourselves but liberating. We would not lightly do such a thing in Holland but once in Germany we considered the enemy fair game. Just think of all the loot they had taken and the damage they had done all over Europe, we told ourselves. It would only be just to give them a taste of their own medicine.

Wearing out collars and ties proudly, though they were far from elegant, Les and I and another gunner whose name I cannot remember went for a stroll around the village. All was quiet. The enemy were the other side of the river and not likely to try to come back: moreover the nearby soldiers were from the Commando Regiment who would brook no nonsense. The place was deserted. The inhabitants had flown. It must have been very difficult for the Dutch or the French to know what to do as the battle rolled near. The civilians had no idea just where a battlefield would develop. Indeed, the military often did not know either. If they stayed put the battle might roll by to be fought a few miles further on. On the other hand their particular village might become a major strongpoint for the defending army and be turned to rubble in a matter of a few days. Anyway the inhabitants of Posterholt had not stayed to find out.

We looked into a house. The door was open. Furniture and furnishings were broken and trampled on. The house must have been fought through. There was a top hat lying on the floor in the hall. Les picked it up, dusted it down and put it on his head at a rakish angle.

'Shall we go to the Dorchester or to Claridges tonight? he asked.

I spotted a cheese cutter and put it on my head. It came down to my ears.

'I think we'll get James to drive us to the Strand Palace.'

Our companion picked up yet another hat, this time a lady's velour.

'No,' he said, 'we will dine at home!'

Laughing and dancing we leapt up on to an embankment surrounding the village and minced along singing and chortling at each other's foolishness.

Suddenly there was a bellow from behind us.

'Take those ridiculous hats off!' A unknown colonel had appeared between the houses and spotted us.

We froze. We doffed our headgear and returned them sheepishly to the trampled house and threw them back on the floor. Still it had been fun, and we heard no more about our prank. Could there be a charge such as wearing unsuitable headgear in a battle zone?

Probably not, but had the senior officer wanted to he could have traced our unit and we could have been charged with conduct prejudicial to good order and military discipline, that good old catch all.

March was occupied in preparing for the assault across the Rhine which in the Dutch area was over a mile wide. This was to be like a miniature Normandy landing again. I was fortunate enough to have ten days' leave in England. This was a privilege possible only for British soldiers whose native land was so near. It was not possible for American soldiers to have any home leave. Those of the Empire and Commonwealth also were too far from home to be able to enjoy such delight. I can recall nothing of that leave except the journey via Calais which had by this time fallen. It was in an awful mess. There were ships sunk in the harbour and the danger of mines was very real. In fact, a troop ship was sunk by a mine as it left Calais whilst I was home on leave. Dover was not much better. There were sunken vessels in the harbour and the town was still showing signs of the bomb and shell damage that it had endured for four long years.

On March 27th the Division began to move across a bridge put up by the engineers to touch land on the eastern bank at Xanten. The main assault had been undertaken by other divisions including 6th Airborne which had landed by parachute and glider at Hamminkeln. Opposition had been fierce. The east bank of the Rhine had been held by some of the toughest and most fanatical German troops. Our role in the campaign was ambiguous. The war was nearly over. It was not likely that our division would ever again meet heavy and co-ordinated mortar attack. The battle was now one of rapid movement into Germany to cut off and destroy the German army in the north and drive to the Elbe to make contact with the Red Army. The army slang word for this kind of advance was "swanning". We were "swanning" as fast as we could into the interior of the Third Reich, because the army was sticking its neck out like a swan in flight. Although counter mortar work was not likely to happen the CMOS was to play a special role in the final stages of the war — two in fact.

In our half-tracks we rolled along with Divisional Headquarters, passing over rubble in shattered villages and halting at the roadside when opposition was met. I remember that there was stiff resistance at the crossroads town of Rheine where there was a cadet training school for the Kriegsmarine, which was the German navy. We passed through wooded country followed by heathland. Most of the farms were small holdings in the style previously met in Holland. Some of the farmers had slave labour to work for them. Some farmers treated them reasonably well. Others regarded them as "untermenschen", that is to say as sub-human. Where they had been reasonably treated the workers, usually Poles, stayed with them. Where they had been badly treated they ran away and took to the woods and begged from the passing British for food. We saw some strange and disturbing sights that were to become magnified as we went further. We met a Frenchman who had been conscripted to work in Germany. He wore his beret at a jaunty angle and was making his way back to France. By his appearance he had been well treated. He knew where he was going. We met others who were ill-kempt, poorly dressed and hungry who were on the road going they knew not where. They were some of a huge army of displaced persons, as officialdom was to label them, which had to be housed and fed in camps by the Allies for years after hostilities had ceased.

The German army was now very disorganised. Higher command had broken down. Many soldiers were deserting, fleeing to the woods, dumping their uniforms and emerging as civilians or slave workers with clothes given to them by sympathetic civilians or stolen from homes sometimes at gunpoint. Other soldiers were regrouped by duty conscious officers and kept in local battle until overwhelmed or by-passed. The nature of the war was very fluid with our units jostling ahead and missing the enemy and leaving pockets behind to fight on or to give themselves up.

There were also escaped Russian prisoners of war dressed in their bottle green who welcomed us with warmth and searched wayside houses for knives and axes with which to arm themselves. They feared for their lives and in turn the German civilians feared for their own lives whilst the Ruskies were around.

One day we were called upon to take on our first new role. I do not know what the other OP and HQ section were doing but Sergeant Lloyd's half-track was ordered to set up a prisoner of war cage.

We pulled in at a farm on the outskirts of a straggling village near some woods. Within half an hour the first German soldiers began to arrive unescorted along the road and out of the woods. Most had been in hiding not knowing how to give themselves up.

Being law abiding and obedient by upbringing, the

Germans knew that they had to surrender to the victorious invaders; besides it was safer to be under the protection of the British lest they were attacked by marauding Russians freed from a nearby prison camp. Within an hour there were thirty of them of all shapes and sizes and services. A tall, immaculate gefreite of the Luftwaffe in what seemed to be a brand new uniform, his bright yellow lapel markings standing out against the blue of the jacket. A young, poorly clad Wehrmacht private, with worn boots, hat too big for him and a pallid, drawn face. He did not look a day over fourteen. A middle-aged captain with white infantry piping who became their natural commanding officer. A lieutenant with red artillery markings. The officers were resigned and co-operative. Indeed all of the prisoners were co-operative even if the Luftwaffe corporal was stiff-necked, arrogant and a pain in the arse to those guarding him. If he did not attempt to run away he moved and reacted to orders given him by his British captors with slow distain. What we would call dumb insolence. It is still a matter of regret forty years on that one of us did not give him a hard shove with the butt end of a rifle.

Sergeant Lloyd and his men were bemused by this sudden and unexpected change of role. How could we guard these men without a perimeter fence? How could we feed them without extra rations? How could we supply them with bedding? Of find water for drinking and washing?

The guarding became easier when a supply truck drove up from nowhere and dumped some reels of barbed wire on the road. We paid out the wire, tearing our hands on the vicious barbs. We needed heavy duty gloves for this work. As if by magic the truck ceased to vanish into the distance and backed down the road to where we were standing examining our hands.

'Here you are mate,' called the driver, 'you'll need these. I almost forgot them'.

We were tossed two pairs of thick, stiff gloves. With these we were able to make a boundary around the farm, hooking the wire on to farm posts and looping it around the twisted iron supports supplied to hold up the wire. We had just enough for a single strand at waist height to complete the boundary.

It would not keep in anyone who wanted to leave. But who wanted to leave?

Our thirty nondescript prisoners were joined by more than a hundred more. Sergeant Lloyd became increasingly worried.

'We can't take anymore, boy,' he confided in me. Sometimes he seemed treat me like a son or a younger brother. 'What can we do if we get anymore? I know they are all surrendering but there's only six of us and we couldn't hold them if they made a charge at us.'

His fears were increased when a further bunch plodded in. 'Where on earth are they all coming from?'

It was clear that troops on the advance had been given orders to point any German soldiers that were giving themselves up in our direction. Sergeant Lloyd's anxiety was partly met by some new arrivals. Six or seven men smartly dressed in brown and white uniforms marched into the farmyard and their leader saluted.

'We are officers and men of the army of the King of Yugoslavia,' he uttered in perfect English.

In bewilderment Sergeant Lloyd returned the salute and walked away. What else could happen? Who else might arrive? A squad from the Waffen SS?

There was a sudden diversion as the farm owner, an elderly woman who could have been taken for a witch in a fairy tale by the Brothers Grimm, went over to the hand pump in the corner of the yard and found it to be broken. There had been some water for the prisoners but not any longer.

'Pump kaput!' She screamed. She shook her fist at us. 'Pump Kaput! Englishen Schweinhunden!'

The tired German captain went over to her to calm her. He told her it was no good complaining. The pump had not been broken on purpose. She continued to mouth her fury and made her way back to the house shaking her fist as she went. The prisoners looked on in dumb silence. They reminded me of a herd of cowed and weary cattle.

We talked with the Yugoslavs. Their senior officer was an amazing man being able to speak seven different languages fluently. We did not succeed in finding out just what they were doing in Germany. It seemed that they had been prisoners of some kind. They had belonged to the Royal army under General Michaelovitch who had fought the Germans first and then Marshal Tito rather than the Germans. In this confusion the British Government had switched support to Tito and his Communist Partisans because they were more effective in fighting the enemy. In retrospect these men now in the farmyard may have been members of a Fascist Croatian Army who had collaborated with the Nazis. Of all these political niceties we knew very little and welcomed these Yugoslavs as being on our side. We enrolled them into our guard duty and lent them rifles when it was their turn to keep an eye on the prisoners.

The prisoners did not like the arrangement at all. They conferred in groups until finally the captain came over to the Sergeant.

'Sergeant, we do not like that we are guarded by these men. We do not recognize them as genuine soldiers. We feel insulted that you have given them guns to guard over us. I wish to make the strongest protest!'

Sergeant Lloyd drew himself up to his full height of five feet three inches and replied, 'We need them. You will have to put up with them. You are in no position to make a complaint.'

The captain returned to his men standing in the damp farmyard as the mists of evening began to gather. He explained the position and shrugged his shoulders. There was nothing to be done. The Germans muttered and scowled but could do little else. They had already decided that the war was over and that they would have to put up with all manner of things that they would find unpleasant.

The prisoners were instructed, using the Yugoslav officer as an interpreter, to pull straw out from the barns to make the farmyard less wet for standing in. At the same time they were encouraged to bed down on the straw left in the barn. As night fell the smell of unwashed bodies slightly alleviated by the strange smell of the ersatz soap and talcum that indicated the presence of German military arose from the barn.

Two Yugoslavs appeared with a pig which they intended to slaughter for their evening meal. After some dissention the would-be butchers were accompanied by Les and myself to the farm kitchen and the witch was summoned. She certainly had spirit. She refused to open the door until we threatened to shoot out the lock. We burst into the kitchen and helped ourselves to two large knives. She must have feared for her life, but we only intended them for the pig.

The pig was hung up by its back legs and its throat was cut. Its squeals could be heard for miles. Eventually the pig was dead and drained of blood. Once this gruesome task was over which appeared to affect the Yugoslavs not in the least, the animal was cut up into large joints and cuts for cooking on a camp fire in the yard. The barn was almost set on fire so large it was and so fiercely did it burn! We were invited to partake of the meal which some of us did although at least two of our six declined being sickened by the butchery. There was nothing for the prisoners except water which had been fetched previously in buckets from the nearest village house.

At midday on the morrow three large trucks arrived with a British officer interpreter. It was not before time since the sanitary arrangements at the farm were non-existent for the numbers that we had to look after. The prisoners were paraded. They stood in several rows weary, hungry and defeated. Even the Luftwaffe corporal looked downcast. The interpreter called them to attention and addressed them briefly. One by one they were ordered on to the awaiting vehicles. The old witch appeared and demanded compensation for the damage done to her farm property.

'Yes, yes,' said the interpreter in her own language. 'You may or may not get compensation. You must claim from the military government once the war is over.'

The trucks drove away somewhere for the prisoners to be identified, listed, numbered, fed and housed. They were not our problem anymore. Our holding operation was over. We received orders to rejoin the CRA. Only the Yugoslavs were left.

'Please do not leave us here,' said their articulate officer. 'We have no arms of our own and we will be attacked by the locals once you are gone. You know how we were hated for guarding the German prisoners. News will get around and we shall be killed!'

The sergeant was in a dilemma. He scratched his head

and said he was sorry but he could not do anything more to help. I suggested that we could take them a mile or two away from the village for their safety and then leave them to fend for themselves.

This was agreed and so we shook hands and Les drove them away as suggested, leaving them a mile or two down the road the way we came earlier. I often wondered what became of them. They would not be welcomed back in Yugoslavia. If they returned they would almost certainly stand trial and be shot by Tito's men.

In fact I was to meet up with more Yugoslavs before I left the army in Germany for good.

Advancing once more with the rest of the Division (we had only been out of the race for a day and a half) we clattered along country roads and through more woodlands and heathland interspersed with small holdings. The countryside was swarming with greenclad Russians, hungry, revengeful and desperate. They would have to be rounded up, brought under control and sent back to their own country, but that was not our job. We had to press on with the Division towards Bremen.

We halted on the outskirts of Bremen. German resistance had hardened once more. There were three incidents worth recording. We met up with a group of Polish farm workers who were now freed from the forced labour. Someone produced a camera, no doubt "liberated" from some house, and several pictures were taken. It seems that I needed a haircut badly according the the photograph. The Poles were delighted to be free again and we were happy to have been instrumental in freeing them. I do not recall seeing any farm owners. I suppose they took refuge in the big farmhouse or had gone with the German forces into Bremen. German civilians in general kept a very low profile at this time. They were in danger of being caught in the centre of a pitched battle, of being attacked by freed foreign workers with a score to settle, of being murdered by Russian released prisoners on the run and of being overrun by the advancing Allies with unforseeable outcomes. On the whole they secretly welcomed the British as they brought with them an assumed sense of fair play and therefore the likelihood of some order and security. The Germans were taught from youth to respect order and authority and they usually got both from the British forces. We had been warned of fanatical German resistance that would be offered by the German underground movement. We were told that there were secret armies of so-called "Werewolves" who would carry out sabotage and assassination once we had occupied the country. We expected this sort of resistance as the Germans themselves had received it from the hands of French, Belgian and Dutch Resistance groups. But this proved to be a non-existent threat. If there were any "Werewolves" about they did not show themselves and soon gave themselves up. Perhaps that forlorn young soldier in our prisoners' cage had been a budding member.

Anyway the expected attacks by a hidden enemy brandishing Spandaus and carrying deadly Panzerfaust anti-tank rockets proved to be a product of Adolf Hitler's imagination.

As we were sunning ourselves with the Polish workers and congratulating ourselves on the expected end of the war, there was the sound of anti-aircraft fire which suddenly began bursting overhead. What on earth was going on? What was being fired at? We soon found out. A large three-engined Junkers 52 transport plane, the sort made of corrugated aluminium, flew ponderously over the trees circling the farm and struggled to keep going at a low altitude with shells bursting all around it and machine gun bullets zipping up from the ground as soldiers became aware of its progress and joined in the attempt to bring it down.

It skimmed the tree tops making a great din and continued on its flight, pursued by the gun fire. Where it was going to and whether it ever got there we never knew. The roar and throb of its engines died away and the gunfire ceased.

The Division was diverted from Bremen which was heavily defended and turned south east. We came across a small town that seemed to be quite deserted. Forward a tank battle was in progress. We stopped and awaited fresh orders. There was a newly built house at the side of the road where we were stationary. It was empty of inhabitants. The door was not locked. Four of us walked in. There was no damage. No one had tried to turn the place over. There had been no looting. Perhaps the occupants had left only within the hour. It was interesting to see what the furnishing of a relatively prosperous German family would be. In the living room there was a pianola. I had never seen one before. The electricity was still working. Clearly the occupants of this house had not been gone long. Someone who had seen a pianola before switched the power on and the roll began to play the piano mechanically filling the room with the strains of a Beethoven sonata. We were surprised and delighted with this new experience. The pianola played on until it came to the end of the roll. Someone looked out of the window to see if we were moving off. The half-track was still there with Sergeant Lloyd looking at the house with an anxious expression.

'Don't worry, Sarge,' we called, 'We'll come as soon as you give the signal.'

The bookcase had a good collection of books on its shelves.

'Hey, look what I've found!' I called, 'It's a copy of *Mein Kampf*.'

I pulled the book out and opened the front cover. It had been awarded to someone, presumably the resident of the house. It was signed by Hitler. I opened a drawer. Lying in it was a red Nazi armband, with the swastika in black on a white background.

Both the book and the armband were legitimate souvenirs. The householders were active party members. No wonder they had made a quick exit! Was there anything else we might take?

'Shoes,' went up the cry.

We raced upstairs and looked under the beds and in the wardrobes for the shoes that we had promised ourselves. I was lucky. I found a pair of good brown shoes that fitted me pretty well. Some of the others were less fortunate.

'Get on board!' came the voice of the sergeant. 'We are moving forward.'

We left the house as quickly as we could. The wardrobe doors were left open but nothing else was touched. Even the electric pianola was switched off. Anyone returning would find little changed and only a book, an armband and three pairs of shoes were missing. We were not being careful for the sake of the residents who we thought to be "bad" Germans, but in case we were caught in the house by our own people and accused of looting which was strictly forbidden and punishable.

Later we were to see signs of wholesale damage and looting but none of us were ever guilty of that.

At a river crossing at a place called Rethem we ran into another battle. A whole trainload of 88mm guns that had been used for anti-aircraft purposes were lined up on a railway siding. They were manned by Kriegsmarine sent out from Hamburg. There were at least eight of these accurate guns and several of a bigger calibre as well on the road. These held our forces up for twenty-four hours. Infantry and tanks were needed to outflank and put them out of action and we stood at readiness in case mortars were to be found. As dusk fell the Luftwaffe came over and bombed and straffed our positions. This was the first time we had met German bombers since the nights at Demouville, though we had seen some German jet fighters in the sky flying incredibly fast. The enemy had beaten the RAF in getting their jets first into operation, and they were much faster than our piston driven Typhoons, Tempests and revamped Spitfires. Our jet, the Meteor, hardly flew before the war had ended. Had the Luftwaffe been able to use its jets a year earlier the campaign in Normandy and beyond might have been rather different. Fortunately the jets were late in operation and the airfields by that time were being rapidly overrun. The Luftwaffe attack at Rethem was nasty but in the nature of a final throw.

At this stage of the war the German forces were being concentrated into smaller and smaller slices of territory being squeezed by the Allies from the west and by the Russians from the east. Consequently the remaining elements of the enemy airforce were compacted together and could put up serious resistance with shortened supply lines and bases nearer to the swiftly advancing Allies.

On the British side there was a notable reluctance to engage the enemy too closely as the end of the war seemed imminent and no one wanted to die within a few days of victory and peace.

Fortunately there was a steadily reducing need to go into a pitched battle. But at Rethem there was strong resistance and some necessary fighting and the Luftwaffe assault was both unexpected and extremely unpleasant. I was more scared at Rethem under air attack than I had been at any previous stage of the campaign. Perhaps it brought back unhappy memories of 1940 when my father had been killed in a daylight raid virtually at my side, and when the raids on London went on night after night through the Autumn and Winter of 1940–41.

Rethem seemed to be the last vicious throw of a defeated enemy as we took cover in a meadow beneath the half-track. The Heinkels rumbled overhead on their bombing run and we wondered where was the RAF. Maybe I had run out of endurance, maybe the war experience banked in my mind was becoming overdrawn.

After Rethem the advance continued with the unexpected always waiting round the corner. It is difficult to convey the chaos that Germany was now in. Not only was there fierce fighting in pockets, sudden swoops forward where the enemy had left gaps, but the countryside was on the move. German soldiers giving themselves up. Slave workers taking to the roads in all directions. Civilian refugees. Former prisoners on the run. A breakdown of central and local government leading to food shortages, news blackouts, rumour upon rumour, and the turning to crime to survive.

There was one unexpected scene that was exciting and emotional. We came across a big prisoner-of-war camp in the woods outside a village called Fallingbostel. Before any of the British army had arrived the German guards had fled and the camp gates were flung open and out poured hundreds of British and Allied prisoners looking for the advancing army. When we came in sight there was such excitement. Cheer upon cheer, tears and laughter. For the prisoners it was a dream come true! Our CMOS unit was not the first to arrive but we were not far behind. A Regimental Sergeant Major had taken over command when the guards left and had begun to organise all the men. There was a shortage of food and some of the men were in a bad way. Some of those freed were former members of the 7th Armoured Division having been taken prisoner at

Villers Bocage in Normandy in the June of the previous year. There were also members of the Airborne Division that had gone into Arnhem and others that had landed on the east bank of the Rhine. The men were left to care for themselves as we swept on towards Soltau, but we learnt that food and newspapers had been sent back to them until arrangements could be made to get them home. The great thing was that they were free!

I shall never forget the excitement as we drove slowly past the camp gates and waved and cheered with all the happy crowd assembled outside to see the liberators pass.

The next day there was fighting for the town of Soltau. There being no concentration of mortars for us to spot we had to wait in the rear. As we drove to find a suitable place to spend the night we were stopped by military police.

'Halt! You cannot come down this road. It is out of bounds.'

Mystified, we halted and turned off the road into a clearing in the woods.

What was going on? Why was the road out of bounds? Always the curious one I asked the Redcaps halting the traffic what all the fuss was about.

'Can't tell you exactly. It's a health hazard.'

What was a health hazard? This titbit of information was merely tantalising. I had to know more. After a while some members of the Pioneer Corps came past looking down and drawn.

'What's going on here?' I asked. 'Have you been involved in this health problem that's stopped us going through the woods?'

'Yeah, and it's a bleeding awful business,' was the first reply.

'They found hundreds of bodies of slave workers in the woods. They had been allowed to die. All skinny and bags of bone they were. They were buried in shallow graves. The local civilians have been made to dig them up and to give them a proper burial.' A more eloquent private filled me in with the information. 'We've had to strip all our clothes off and be fumigated in case we carried any infection with us. And there's still more to be buried tomorrow.'

Was this the notorious concentration camp at Belsen? Or

was it a separate, smaller scale model of enemy barbarity? I believe that it was Belsen and that the bodies in the wood were only the beginning of the fearful discovery to be made. Certainly anyone who had been in that prohibited area and had been engaged in dealing with the dreadful problems encountered looked as if they had been to hell and spent a lifetime there.

On our advance to Hamburg we passed along an autobahn that ran through heathland and small woods of pine. Several attacks were made on the moving columns by German fighter jets. I took several photographs of one straffing raid from a ditch. The film developed all right but so great was the speed of the aircraft that it appears as a blur. Once again I have no recollection of where I obtained the camera or how I later got the film developed. On each side of the autobahn and deep into the heath were large enemy dumps of shells and bombs and petroleum. Care was needed in driving off the road. We came to an abandoned air base and gingerly explored some of the huts for souvenirs. The equipment was superb. Every weapon, every tool, every piece of motor transport was excellently made and extremely functional. In the profession of war the Germans were past masters in getting the right thing made at the right time to the right specification. We and the Americans outclassed them in sheer volume but were invariably less than leaders in technology. Only in our artillery and in our radar and radio equipment were the Allies superior.

This may seem a very sweeping statement and may not have been true of the air forces or the navy. But the impression we all got in Europe was that the German army was very well equipped and efficient and needed superior numbers to overcome them. Thank God for the superior numbers!

I mentioned earlier that our unit was to have two unusual roles to play. One was to set up a temporary POW cage which I have already written about in this chapter. The other was to take over and guard Hamburg Airport. The war was about to end. Negotiation for the surrender of Hamburg had been completed. Our two half-tracks were ordered to enter the airport and ensure that no acts of sabotage took place. Somewhat overwhelmed with our orders we drove up to the gates. They were opened by airport police, armed we noticed with neat Luger pistols, who saluted smartly and let us through. The police were dressed in light green uniforms with those strange leather helmets rather like our postmen wore in the 1920s. They were asked to hand over their weapons which they did somewhat reluctantly. The next day a staff officer drove up and demanded that the police be given back their pistols. It seemed that the senior British officer who had accepted the surrender of the city had agreed that the police be allowed to keep their small arms otherwise they, the police, could not guarantee to keep order in the city. So the two sergeants of our unit had to be found and ordered to hand over their coverted Lugers. They were even more reluctant to hand them back than the police had been to hand them over on the previous day!

As part of our duties of guarding the airport we thought we had better search every building. So for several mornings and one or two afternoons we went through hangars and workshops. The airport was large and had been used for military as well as civilian purposes. As we went about our task German Focke-Wolfe fighters flew in from time to time and landed near the control tower. The pilots clambered out of their planes and walked straight into the foot of the control tower. We made no move to stop or question them, and never saw them again once they were into their mess. No doubt others were responsible for them. We were only non-commissioned army types. The pilots were responding to a call for all German airforces to surrender and fly their machines to the nearest airbase occupied by the Allies. The war was not yet officially over but the ceasefire announcement could not be long delayed now.

The exploration of the hangers and sheds around the airport perimeter was absorbing. We felt like little boys scrumping apples with the farmer safely away. In one hanger was a Heinkel 111, one of the bombers, no doubt, that had attacked us at Rethem. The Heinkel 111 had also figured prominently in the Blitz on Britain. By 1944 it was rather out-dated being no match for the Allied fighters. We

Hamburg Airport, May 1945
left, Sgt. Lloyd, centre, the author, right, Denis Bould and Buck.

climbed into the machine and explored the cockpit, the rear gunner's position, the bomb aimer's position and the various pieces of equipment. As those who had been at the receiving end of this carrier of death we were very interested to see how it felt from the inside. It was very cramped, as bad if not worse than being cooped up in a tank. To get into the tail gunner's position was a work of art worthy of a flexible sardine. We scrambled out glad that we were not German bomber crews. In another hangar was a ME 110, a fighter bomber. We did not explore this closely as it seemed to have bombs in its bomb racks and we feared the possibility of a booby-trap. In every building we searched for weapons. Everyone was looking for a Luger, the souvenir symbol of that time. We did not find any, but I picked up a Beretta machine pistol and a small Italian automatic. The former I handed in, but the latter I kept with twenty rounds of ammunition. This was to be an object of admiration for some but also a vehicle of near disaster subsequently.

There was time on our hands. I cannot remember anything about our eating arrangements but I suppose our own cooks collected rations from a supply unit somewhere. I have several photographs taken of our unit on the aerodrome. There is one with Sergeant Lloyd and a couple of us taken in front of a Focke-Wolfe fighter. How proud we were at having come so far and having our picture taken in front of the spoils of war. To think that the mighty German war machine had been finally brought to a standstill and a defeat by overwhelming occupation. It still seemed a dream.

Then we got the word to go again. We crossed the Elbe and drove through devastated Hamburg. The docks and steel works were twisted steel girders and piles of rubble. The streets were lined with rubble, cleared to make a way for the convoy by pale and poorly dressed civilians. It was not only the slave workers that looked under-nourished. As we drove up through Holstein toward the Keil Canal we passed hundreds of German soldiers trudging south to give themselves up in Hamburg. We took very little notice of them and they took even less notice of us. It was no time for jeering. We had all seen enough of war for that. The enemy soldiers were dust-stained and silent. Amongst the foot-sloggers were some large diesel wagons heavily loaded with men, and some horsedrawn vehicles. They were probably glad it was all over for them and that they had been taken by the British and not by the Russians.

Just outside Itzehoe, a town distinguished by its cement factories, we halted and turned into a field.

'Grub up!' came the cry after an hour of preparation. The afternoon sun began to sink slowly to the west. It was May 6th and we heard on the radio that all hostilities had ceased. The surrender of the German army had been officially signed on Luneburg Heath. There was no holding us. A group decided to drive up to the Keil Canal just to have a look and to be able to say they had seen it. Two truck loads took off and drove up to the canal cheering. There it was, just a canal, with two gun emplacements guarding the bridge over it.

'Lets go on to Flensburg.' said one.

'What's the point of going to Flensburg?' said another. 'Why not drive up into Denmark, it can't be far away.'

But the most insistent said, 'Let's get back to camp before it gets too dark to find our way and have some drinks.'

And this proved to be the majority opinion.

On the way back several of the lads were determined to force their way into a German house and demand drinks to celebrate the victory. I felt uneasy over this not knowing what might develop. However the driver of the truck was the most determined to carry out this diversion and so willy-nilly we arrived at the door of a farmhouse. The door was knocked on heavily.

'Open up, we're English soldiers. Englishen soldaten. Verstehen Sie?'

The door opened slowly to reveal a very nervous farmer.

The crowd pushed into the small entrance hall.

'Bringen-Sie wein und glasses. What the hell is the German for glasses?'

None of us seemed to know. The ringleaders forced open the door into the parlour. Behind the table stood the farmer's wife looking terrified and suspecting the worst. So, too was her husband.

'Shush!' He entreated, 'Kinder schlaffen.' And he pointed up to the ceiling to indicate that his children were asleep upstairs. I could feel that some of our companions were aroused by the sight of the woman. The situation became increasingly tense.

Glasses were brought and a bottle of wine. The wine was poured.

'Here is a toast,' cried the driver, his eyes on the woman, 'Victory to the British army and to hell with Hitler. Drink!' He commanded the German couple.

They obediently drank literally shaking as they did so. Were they to be murdered? Was the wife to be raped?

'More wine!' commanded the driver, his eyes riveted on the housewife.

'Shush,' said the man, in an agony of apprehension, 'My children.'

'Never mind about your bleeding children, more wine, more wine, schnell!'

More wine was produced and poured. I looked around at the six soldiers squeezed into the small room. How many felt as I did that it was time to go?

'Come on,' I said, 'You've had your fun. Let's leave them in peace. They've got youngsters in bed asleep. Let's get back to our camp.'

'No, not yet,' growled the driver, 'I want more wine and another toast.'

With luck I thought we might get him away. It did not seem that many of the others were determined on rape and pillage.

'Drink to the end of the Nazis and may all frauleins be willing,' leered the driver.

'Okay, let's head for home' said another lad, 'John's right, we've had our fun. Enough is enough.'

We pushed the driver out of the door protesting. 'You silly, weak-kneed buggers. We could all have had a screw of that bint.'

'Yes, I expect you are right, but we're going back to base now and don't crash the truck!'

The driver was not very steady but got into the vehicle and pulled out his rifle.

'I'll put a couple of shots through his window. I'll teach him to have a beautiful wife.'

'Don't be a bloody fool. Do you want to have the blood of innocent children on your hands?'

Slowly the driver put his rifle down. Still protesting he engaged gear and we regained the road.

Once back in our field a sight met our eyes. Several of the men were lying drunk and unconscious in the grass being gently covered with the dew. Amongst them was one of our sergeants. One man was steadily firing his Sten gun in the air and uttering a series of cowhand "whoopies" as he fired. We all joined in with our weapons shooting them off into the night air like Afghan tribesmen.

Across the road was a field with a large haystack in it.

'Come on, lads, let's have a victory bonfire.'

The haystack was lit and a dozen or more soldiers danced round it. In the excitement I flung my fore and aft cap into the air and then into the fire. 'Look,' I cried, 'I've burnt my cap to celebrate victory tonight!'

It seems silly now but it seemed absolutely right at the time, and I was relieved that we had extricated ourselves from a potentially horrific situation in the farmhouse. In the morning there were a number of sore heads including that of the officer commanding, who had locked himself in his caravan and drunk himself into a stupor. The telephone wires were hanging in tatters where the victory salvoes of the night before had shot off.

The next day we were cleaning up, washing the vehicles and generally making do and mend. After our midday meal some of us gathered round to yarn. I produced the automatic pistol that I had found in the airport and showed it to my companions.

'You are sure it's not loaded?' asked one of the bombardiers.

'Yes,' I replied, 'I'm quite sure of that.'

I pulled the trigger to prove it, the muzzle pointing to the bombardier's stomach. There was a click which proved my point.

'You should never point a gun at anyone whether it is loaded or not. You know how that has been drummed into us ever since we have been in the army,' remonstrated one of my pals.

'You are right,' I said, and turning away I pointed the gun to a space between the group and pulled the trigger again. There was a sharp retort and a bullet winged its way into the bushes.

'You bloody fool, you could have killed me,' shouted the bombardier.

Shamefaced, I apologised and walked to the edge of the field and flung the offending gun into the thick hedgerow. I had been lucky once again or was providence looking after me? I had certainly learned my lesson over guns. Had I shot the innocent bombardier in the stomach I would have been on a court martial and almost certainly have spent a spell in military prison. The authorities were hot on possession of illegal arms. How stupid I had been.

The next day we moved to the club house at Wedel.

9

The British Occupation including Berlin

When we drove to the club house in Wedel we realised that we were in luck and very good luck at that. I do not know what club it was whose members had lavished so much money on. It was called Fahrhaus Schulau. Probably it was a yachting fraternity for the club house was situated on the bank of the Elbe. It was on the east bank to be precise where the river was about two miles wide not far from its entrance into the North Sea. It thus lay downstream from Hamburg, on an estuary, in a very pleasant part of the Holstein peninsula.

Each of us had an individual bed, two or three beds to a room, with several washbasins and a shower unit. The kitchens were like those of a hotel and the staff was still there. There was a large bar and a comfortable lounge. It was in immaculate condition.

There was a general order that there should be no fraternisation with the German people. It was permissible to ask for directions, to seek information or to give orders but no one was to develop a friendly relationship. This meant that any meeting with the opposite sex was to be illicit unless through the means of a recognised brothel, or that sexual relationships were to be developed with non-German women. This put the Polish, Czech, Baltic and other foreign nationals at a premium. But it did not follow that they were willing to be free with the British soldiery.

There was a small German boy who used to hang about outside the club and press photographs of his sister into anyone's hand who would take them. I was sufficiently naive to take one of these and wonder why I had been given it. The photograph showed a girl of about sixteen of the most unprepossessing appearance that I had ever seen. She was indeed ugly. I suppose using her young brother as a pimp was the only way that she could win men to her. I showed the photo to one of the older men.

'Throw it away,' he advised. 'She is probably full of VD, and if some of the men catch it from her and go sick we may all be investigated. If that photo was to be found on you then you could be in trouble.'

Although this was probably an exaggeration I needed no encouragement to dispose of the hideous picture. I wonder if she got any customers? Certainly I was confirmed in my view to keep away from all floosies.

There was another way to begin fraternisation. In our wanderings along the edge of the river, Dennis and I had come across some boatmen working on repairs. As we approached one of them he looked up and beckoned us over. Somewhat warily we went up to the man. He was in late middle age with a weather-beaten face and only one arm. He spoke in halting English.

'I was a member of the Social Democratic Party in Germany,' he said softly. 'Spent some time in a concentration camp. You see this arm? I lost it in the last war.'

We moved closer. This was interesting. Was he one of the "good" Germans we had heard about?

'Come for a sail on the Elbe with me. I want you to meet some of my friends. I want you to meet a particular friend who wants to meet an English soldier.'

We nodded. How could we do this?

Back at the club house we put our brains to work. We will ask Lieutenant Hopper, our new second-in-command to authorise our sailing trip as part of an intelligence gathering exercise.

I still have the passes one of which I reproduce below:

922283 L/Bdr Bould has permission to be absent from his unit from 0630 hours 8 July 45 for the purpose of sailing on the R. Elbe.

R.W. Hopper Lt RA
CMO 7 ARMD DIV.

7 July 45

Dennis and I set off early that July morning and met our German "friend" at his harbour. He had a smart little sailing boat with a foresail and a mainsail schooner-rigged. The wind was brisk and the estuary quite choppy. With skill the yachtsman tacked across the wide river, indicating the sandbanks which were exposed when the tide was running out, and headed for the far bank. Once under the lee of the west bank the river was calmer and we sailed along for some time. We were intrigued with the constant sound of bells ringing from within the orchards that covered the west bank.

'They sound like temple bells,' remarked Dennis, 'Surely there aren't any temples in Germany?.'

I was about to say that nothing would surprise me any more when our yachtsman cut in.

'The bells that you can hear are from the cherry orchards. They are used by the fruit farmers to scare the birds away. You know it is here that the big, black cherries are grown. You know we used to send a lot to England before the war. Exports.'

After a while we came to a jetty and the boat was hauled to and tied up. A uniformed man came down to meet us. Our yachtsman spoke to him rapidly in German and we were welcomed ashore. It was obvious that they were acquaintances.

'This way, we have a little walking to do.'

We were led from the riverside along a leafy lane through the orchards to the pleasant accompaniment of the tinkling bells. The sun shone and I felt fit and happy after the sail in the wide estuary.

'You don't think we are being led into some kind of trap,' suggested Dennis.

I said that I was sure we were not being led into any such thing. As usual my curiosity was thoroughly aroused.

At the end of the lane we turned into a dirt road where some pleasant houses and bungalows had been built. At the end was a larger bungalow. We halted at the garden gate.

'Wait here a moment,' said our leader. 'I will see if he is in.'

Who was this person wanting to see us? Could it be some notorious Nazi waiting to give himself up? We had no weapons with us. Had we been wise after all to come on this expedition?

Our yachtsman returned with a broad smile.

'Ja, he is in. Please come this way.'

The front door was open and we were shepherded through the hall into the parlour which was heavily furnished with Nineteenth Century bric-a-brac. There was the smell of old furnishings and stale tobacco smoke. An elderly man was standing by the empty fireplace with two women at his side. One seemed to be his wife, the other his daughter.

'My friends,' said our sailor, 'Allow me to present Herr Schmidt and his family.'

The elderly man bowed and extended his hand to us. Somewhat gingerly we shook it in turn. With tears in his eyes and in a voice shaking with emotion he said in a thick English accent, creaky for lack of use.

'I wish to apologise for all the bad things that my country has done under Hitler. He has ruined our beloved land and made the name of Germany one to be reviled and hated.'

By the time he finished these words he was sobbing and turned his head away with embarrassment.

One of the women said, 'You must forgive my father. He was in the German Foreign Service before World War One. He was a loyal servant of His Imperial Majesty Kaiser Wilhelm the Second. He has hated the Nazis and what they have done.'

We looked at each other and nodded in our own embarrassment. So this was why we had been brought to the other side of the Elbe. To receive a formal apology from an old servant of Imperial Germany.

Having recovered a little the old gentleman turned and took down some framed documents from the high mantle-piece.

'Look, I was the German Consul in Costa Rica in 1908 and I was charged with looking after British interests as well as German. And look here I was also responsible jointly for German and British nationals in Honduras in 1912. We were allies in those days. It was an honour to serve King George as well as the Kaiser.' And another burst of emotion swept over him. His frail shoulders shook.

Emotions were calmed and a bottle and glasses appeared. We drank to the past and to previous Anglo-German friendship. We drank to the future and to renewed Anglo-German friendship. Medals were produced and shown with pride to illustrate the ex-official's credentials. They all dated from pre-1914. There was more hand shaking and more bowing and a further round of schnapps. We left in a slight haze, not knowing if we had over-done the acceptance of the apologies, not knowing if we had exceeded the bounds of the official non-fraternisation orders.

But we knew that the little ceremony had meant much to the frail old gentleman, and also to our yachtsman. He seemed pleased that his task had been accomplished.

'He will die in peace now.'

This was more than we could emotionally handle. We kept silent for some time. When we got back to the club house the lads were more sceptical.

'I bet he didn't make a fuss when Hitler was winning the war for Germany and for him.'

'He's like all the bloody Germans. When they are on top they kick your face in. When they are down they lick your bloody boots.'

But it was not like that with those people we had been with.

Before we left the Elbe for a more exciting situation Dennis and I managed to hire a large rowing boat from one of our sailor's friends and to get some of our pals to help us crew it. Jim Pearce (another Jim Pearce not related in any way to the one in 274 Battery) and George Laidlaw were two of our crew. We were six in all. The rowing was done with four oars, two each side. One man was helmsman and the other at look out. It was grand to move across the wide river going downstream with the tide. We reached the east bank, clambered out of the boat and stretched our legs. We were far from the spot where Dennis and I had landed some days earlier. After a while of sunning ourselves and resting from our unaccustomed labours we got back in and shoved off for the return trip.

All went well until we realised that instead of coming back with the tide as we had hoped the river was still running low and it would be several hours before the tide would turn to our advantage. In mid-stream we hit our first sandbank. The keel of the boat scraped along the sand and slowed us without bringing us to a stop. When we hit the next sandbank, however, the boat stopped.

'Push off!' shouted the helmsman. We put our oars into the water and pushed and pushed. Slowly the boat moved off the bank. On we rowed gathering speed. The west bank looked a long way away. We were in mid-stream. Then we hit the third sandbank. The boat stopped. We pushed and pushed. There was no movement.

'Get into the water and push the boat!' yelled the helmsman. To set the example he pulled off his boots and socks and jumped on to be followed by two others. Thus lightened and encouraged by the brawn of three soldiers the craft slipped slowly forward. Hastily the paddlers dived back into the boat as the sandbank came to an end and deep water was encountered once more.

When we hit our fourth sandbank we knew the drill. Men overboard; push; row; push and back into the boat.

But when we met the next one there was deadlock. Nothing would move the craft off the bank. The water level was still falling. A feeling of panic seized us.

'For God's sake we've got to get off this bank or we shall be marooned for hours. Look, our landing place is over a mile away.'

We could see the little harbour. But how to get to it?

'Everyone into the water. We've got to pull the thing off the sand.'

So there we were up to our knees in water heaving at the boat with all our might. An oar slipped into the water and began to float away.

'Get that oar somebody!'

Somebody splashed after it and went up to his neck in the water. The sand was soft and oozy to the feet. It was not very clean. The man with the oar struggled back to firmer footing and in doing so lost hold of the oar. It drifted slowly away beyond reach.

'Bloody hell, we'll have to pay for that.'

Fortunately the weather was good. The sun shone. Our bare backs were to suffer during the next few days. At last the boat was free of the accursed sand and all regained the safety of the boat. The remaining oars were replaced in the rowlocks, a spare was found for the lost one and the boat's crew, weary but happier directed their craft towards the harbour, and after a steady row against the tide which made progress slowly and made every muscle ache, safety was reached. The owner was not pleased with having his boat returned less one oar, but we paid him what he asked and departed to the club house for food and rest. Our moments of panic were soon forgotten. On the following day we heard that we were going to Berlin.

This was sensational news. The Russians had captured Berlin several weeks before and had advanced up to the Elbe at Magdeburg. The capital city, therefore, lay in the Russian zone of occupation and the Western Allied powers demanded the right to have an occupation zone within Berlin. Much diplomatic discussion had taken place since the end of the war to allow this to happen. At last the decision reached at Yalta had been worked out in detail and the British Zone was to be in the north and west of the city. And 7th Armoured Division was to be assigned the honour of being the first British troops in Berlin!

On July 14th the HQRA, to which we were attached, moved through the Russian Zone to enter the city. The Russians were very suspicious of all their Allies, having been brought up on a diet of spy stories and anti-capitalist propaganda for a generation. The column was not to stop anywhere on the autobahn joining Magdeburg and Berlin. The scenery was one of unrelieved heathland with never a village or sign of occupation in sight. We saw neither German nor Russian until we reached Berlin itself. As we entered the outer suburbs we came to a sign that had been erected by our advance column that had come to the city a week earlier.

It said: "THIS AXIS HAS BEEN LAID FROM EL ALAMEIN TO BERLIN"

It also showed the major battles that the Division had fought on the way and it was illustrated by the divisional sign of the jerboa, the desert rat.

We occupied empty apartments in the suburb of Spandau. We had little to do but clean our equipment, smarten ourselves up in general, scrub and whiten our webbing and have a military presence in the city. In those early days of Allied occupation all zones were freely open for all troops. A big Naafi was opened in the British zone and called the Winston Club. Into this canteen used to flock British, American, French and Russian soldiers for "char" and "wads" (tea and sandwiches).

We were very interested in the Russian soldiers since they were an unknown quantity and also because they were held in great esteem by the Allies on account of their great fight against the Nazis. There was tremendous goodwill between the Allies and the Russians at that time. Goodwill, which unfortunately, was soon to be dissipated by the politicians.

I met one private in the Red Army, very smartly dressed, who spoke good English. He was, in fact, a Pole who had joined the Red Army and had been on the personal staff of a general in command of an infantry division. They had marched all the way from Stalingrad to Berlin, fighting fiercely as they came, a distance of something like one thousand, three hundred miles. They had little transport and made use of what abandoned or captured German equipment they could. This Pole was a linguist as had been the Yugoslav officer. The Pole could speak Polish, Russian, English and German. We were all very impressed. Other Russian soldiers were less impressive. All except senior officers wore a smock over their trousers, a belt and strong leather boots, not unlike German jackboots. They wore peaked caps or fore and aft hats, not unlike our own. Officers and men mixed together more informally than did ours. The officers wore shoulder tabs with their arm and rank indicated in gold on red. Once on duty their discipline was harsh. They had long hours on guard and any slackness was severely punished. Death was not an uncommon sentence for what in our army would have been a relatively mild offence. I thought of my sleeping on duty on more than one occasion and felt glad I had not served in the Red Army.

On one occasion, however, I witnessed an incredible incident. In one of the main streets of the city a Russian jeep pulled up at the side of the road and an officer alighted and entered a building. A few moments later he re-emerged and climbed into the jeep. He lit a cigarette. His driver, who had sat waiting for the officer, leant across the wheel and after a few moments of altercation snatched the cigarette from the officer's mouth and began to smoke it himself! Whereupon the officer snatched it back again and offered a cigarette from his packet to his driver. They then drove away without another word!

Once when it was my tour of duty to be driver for the CMOS I was travelling along a road with burnt out buildings on each side. As I neared an intersection I spotted a Red Army private staggering from side to side. He was obviously very drunk. I halted the truck and called out to him in my poor German if I could take him anywhere. German was the "lingua franca" in Berlin. Only in German could British and Russians make any kind of conversation. He lurched aboard and sat himself down in the passenger seat.

'Ja, Bahnhof.'

I indicated that I wanted to see his papers that he was clutching in his hand.

He had a fist full of Russian banknotes and a pass. I examined the pass trying to find which railway station he wanted. Of course, the pass was made out in Russian. I could make no attempt to read it.

The man took out a bottle of vodka from his pocket (he had another sticking out of his pack), and offered me a drink. Having wiped the bottle neck I obliged him with a swig. I passed back the bottle and began to drive to where I thought the nearest main line terminus was.

'Ich gehe heimat, hic,' he said. 'Ich gehe nach hause. Nach meine mutter und mein vater.'

'You are being demobbed?'

'Ich gehe nach hause, hic. Seit drei jahren ich habe soldaten sein.'

I asked him where he lived. He said near Moscow. So he had been paid off, given a pass and he had to find his own way home the best he could. Well, that was a revelation. Compare that with our meticulous movement orders, our ticket, pass, train itinerary, pick-up and put down points.

I stopped near to a terminus and bade him farewell. We shook hands and he warmly embraced me. He smelt of vodka embibed over many days.

Berlin, the ruin of the Reichstag, note the 88 mm gun.

'Tovarich. Comrade. Kamerad.'

We parted, he near to tears, me not sorry to get rid of him. I hoped that I had stumbled across the right railway station and that trains to the east were actually running.

The centre of Berlin was in a devastated state. Grand official buildings, hotels, department stores and apartments were in ruins or starkly burnt out. Not only had the Germans and Russians fought over the city, block by block, but there had been many heavy bomber raids for several years.

As duty driver I had the opportunity to drive around a little. I found the famous street Unter den Linden and the Wilhemstrasse. Somewhere in the Wilhelmstrasse was the Reich Chancellery, where Hitler had his official residence when in Berlin.

With Dennis and George, I drove the duty truck up to the entrance of the Chancellery. A Russian sentry saluted from a sentry box. We got out of the truck and returned the salute. The sentry did not attempt to stop us. We were British soldiers arriving in a military vehicle therefore we must be authorised to enter the building. In the courtyard was the burnt out remains of a German scout car. We crunched across broken glass and debris and entered the main doors. Where did we go now? From the entrance hall rose a wide and elegant staircase. The walls were pitted with bullet marks and the smell of brick and cement dust hung heavily although the fighting for the building had ceased seven weeks earlier.

At the top of the stairs was a corridor leading from the landing. At the end of the corridor was a large double-door. We pushed the door open and entered. We were in the famous hall of mirrors which I had seen on the newsreel so many times. This was where Hitler had received Mussolini, where Hitler had entertained Molotov and where so many diplomats and statesmen had flitted across the newsreels in the last ten years.

But it was not an elegant reception hall any longer. The mirrors which were fitted to the walls from top to bottom were smashed to the ground and trampled under foot. The Russian soldiers upon entry had fired their Tommy guns all along the walls bringing down glass and plaster. At the far end of the hall was another double door. We opened them and found ourselves in Hitler's study!

There was his large desk empty of all papers and covered in dust. A large and ornamental chandelier hung low from the ceiling. Beyond the desk was a broad window through which could be seen a courtyard. It was Hitler's study for sure, because we all recognised it from newsreel and pictures in the papers. To think that here until a few weeks ago Adolf Hitler had planned and plotted, seen scores of fellow Nazis, received visitors, employed secretaries and written countless war directives. Here had been Hermann Goering, Rudolf Hess, Doctor Goebbels and many other infamous Nazi leaders. We moved to the window and looked out into the courtyard. It was quite small. A brick wall some twelve feet high surrounded it. In one corner was the remains of a large bonfire. The wall was smoke-blackened by its burning. We left the room feeling exultant. We had got to the heart of the Third Reich.

We walked along other corridors and into a succession of offices. Here the numerous secretaries had typed and filed and noted the commands of the Fuhrer. Ranged along the walls and jutting out into the offices was filing cabinet upon filing cabinet of personnel. We opened them at random. There were cards of party members neatly filed and indexed. I took one as a souvenir, now lost these many years. Maybe he was a much wanted war criminal and I inadvertantly allowed his records to vanish. One shelf had a stack of cards inviting someone to have breakfast with the Furher. The name was left blank for insertion but the time was printed in black on yellow "10.00". We helped ourselves to some of these. What a hoot it would be to say that we had been invited to have breakfast with Hitler! As a final memento I helped myself to a typewriter brush with the obscure reason that it would remind me of our adventure each time that I cleaned my webbing equipment. On the way out we paused at a small doorway that must have led into the basement. Should we go down and explore further? We did not have a torch and, furthermore, there might be a booby trap. A vision of a deadly Panzerfaust primed to blow our heads off when the door was opened made us draw back. So we walked away from the basement where had we known was the war operations suite of Hitler — his underground bunker where he spent his last days, married Eva Braun and finally shot himself.

All that was yet to be discovered and his last days reconstructed by Hugh Trevor-Roper in his book '*The Last Days of Hitler*'.

The smoke-blackened courtyard was where Hitler's body had been burned after his suicide by his last devoted guards. We had seen this and not realised at the time its significance.

When I returned some days later with some other soldiers to do some further exploring and take some photographs there were British military police on guard with the Russians and we were turned away.

'No, admittance only to intelligence officers and officers above the rank of Major.'

So that was it! Major Trevor-Roper was doing his detective work. But we, a Lance Bombardier and two gunners had got in there before him!

Berlin had been a beautiful city. It was now a ruin and in economic and social chaos. Food was desperately short for the civilians. The value of money had plummeted to zero. The means of exchange was the cigarette. Every day a Black Market congregated near to the Brandenburg Gate. There the Berliners would come with their surviving possessions and trade them for cigarettes. A camera would be bartered for fifty cigarettes, a gold wrist watch for forty, binoculars would go for twenty. A woman's body could be had for ten cigarettes, or better still become a soldier's lover for as long as he was in Berlin for this ensured food and protection. For the Berliners feared the Russians and almost regarded the British as saviours. In fact more than one British Tommy shacking up with his fraulein was heard to say, 'We fought the wrong war. We should have been on the Germans' side against the Ruskies.'

But that was the result of pillow talk and a concern for a lover who was in very real fear of the Red Army. The non-fratenisation order was speedily eroded and after several months was revoked.

There were other pastimes for the British soldier. A series of lakes lay to the west of the city. These had been pleasure resorts for the Berliners. Now they were put at the disposal of the occupying forces. Dennis and I spent many happy hours on the lakes. We went canoeing in a kayak and soon mastered the double-sided paddles. Had we not mastered the Elbe with oars? A steam driven lake steamer chugged its way across the largest lake filled with boozy soldiers, singing and laughing. The German operators and the staff of the lakeside club that had been re-opened for our men seemed to enjoy our good spirits as much as we did. I suppose that they were used to seeing their own young men doing the same thing. Every German loves a soldier, or they used to!

There was a rumour that in a tunnel between two subway stations in the centre of the city lay several hundred dead SS soldiers who had fought to the last and then retreated there. The Russians had blocked any escape along the tunnels and entombed them. Whether this was true or not, none of the underground trains were running and in certain places in the city the smell of death was strong. This was made worse by the July weather which was exceptionally hot. The tar melted in the streets under the blazing sun.

One evening as we came out of the Catholic soldiers club near to one of the main line stations, we saw some emaciated German soldiers standing at the corner of the road. They were in tattered Wehrmacht uniforms and their boots were worn right through. One of them was barefooted with straw wrapped round his bleeding feet. My anger at what the Germans had done to people of other countries and the appalling way the Nazis had acted towards the Jews evaporated at the sight of these men. They had obviously been on the Russian Front and had been prisoners and were now released to get home however best they could. The Russians could hardly treat their bitter enemies better than they treated their own men released from military service.

'Look at those half-starved Jerries. They're skin and bone. What do you say to buying some food at the canteen and giving it to them?'

My companions were uncertain.

'Suppose some one sees us we might get into trouble.'

'Why should we get into trouble? Come on I'm going to get something for them.'

Only one of my two companions joined me. The other looked on disapprovingly.

We got some doughnuts and took them over to the gaggle of men. They took them and thanked us and wolfed them eagerly. We never saw them again.

Another activity that I got myself engaged in was a forces newspaper. A fellow gunner called Peter Boot had been a trainee journalist and we, together with another soldier, Wally Coldrick, who had been with me in 274 Battery and who had been a commercial artist, were encouraged by the Brigadier (the CRA) to set up the weekly paper. Boot proved to be a whizz kid in locating German printers and paper wholesalers. We decided to call our paper *The Berlin Bugle*. In our first edition there was a brilliant cartoon executed in the style of Giles. It showed two husky, macho soldiers (like Bluto in Popeye) looking at a poster advertising entertainments. One says to the other, 'What shall it be tonight Beethoven, ballet, booze or bints?'

Bints was the current term for girls.

We found some pin-ups of German girls and had them

The black market in Tiergarten.

put in: one per edition. They were quite daring for the time but nothing like Penthouse. We interviewed various officers and other ranks, and wrote up the interviews for the paper. I have several editions of *The Bugle* in front of me now. The first page of the first edition ran the following story with two small photographs.

BLACKMARKET BOOMS IN BERLIN

Berlin's "Petticoat Lane"

Thousands of Cigarettes and bars of chocolate change hands for films, cameras, watches, rings, silver cutlery, binoculars, pens and even piano accordians.

*By J.P. Meot**

Hearing so much about Berlin's blackmarket, a party of the editorial staff set off in a jeep, complete with camera

---

* Nom-de-plume for Mercer and Boot.

The massed bands of the Scottish Divisions playing in Potsdam Strasse, Berlin in July 1945.

and notebooks to get the real lowdown on this illegal trading.

Arriving at one of the blackmarket centres, we nearly caused a riot, as only the night before there had been a raid by military and civilian police. Buyers and sellers had been caught and taken in charge. When the crowd saw our jeep with the big notice "FORCES NEWSPAPER" stuck on the front, and our party with notebooks and camera, they naturally thought it was another raid. As soon as they saw that we were quite harmless — trade restarted.

As this centre was well within the British Zone, it was not subject to the hordes of American and Russians, thus keeping prices reasonably low. All transactions were done quite openly. The German civilians walked slowly around the square holding their wares conspicuously. The "swaddies" move equally slowly eyeing their retailers carefully.

A transaction was in progress between a well-dressed young woman speaking passable English, who was trying to sell a folding camera for two hundred cigarettes, and a gunner. As soon as they began to inspect the article, crowds of would-be customers and rival sellers gathered round. Advice is offered in loud tones from both German and English spectators.

The camera was inspected, the lense checked. "Okay", said the buyer, "two hundred fags" — and so the trade went on.

One hundred marks is the ceiling price for ten cigarettes. 5/– a fag in England will be the time to stop smoking! The Germans must imagine we each own a chocolate factory. One man wanted thirty bars for his camera.

BUT — In one day last week sixteen Russian officers were court-martialled and 2,000 civilians arrested. The British and Americans, too are tightening up. So beware Gunner Brown!'

One of the great events in Berlin was an inter-allied athletics meeting in the Olympic Stadium. This was the one where the black Jesse Owens defeated the German sprinters and caused Hitler much displeasure in 1936. The following is a report on the inter-allied event as reported in *The Bugle.*

ALLIED SPORTS IN OLYMPIC STADIUM

USA wins by long lead

Competitors from the Berlin Forces of the United States, France and Great Britain held a big athletic meeting in the Olympic Stadium last Sunday, 23rd September '45. Red Army athletes were to, have attended, but they were withdrawn at the last moment.

Memories of the pre-war Olympic Games were

awakened when the meeting was opened by a parade of those taking part. The British competitors led dressed in white flannels and singlet, followed by the Americans clad in blue zipped track suits (shades of the APTC) and finally the French in khaki green trousers and white singlets.

The Stadium was well filled and the athletes received a good round of applause. Throughout the afternoon bands of the three Allied nations played. As usual camera enthusiasts were to the fore. The supply of film seems to be unceasing.

From the beginning America took the lead and early in the events it was apparent that neither Britain nor France would regain it. Sgt. Watkins, USA, took the high jump with apparent ease at 194cms. The 3,000 metres (7 and a half times round the track) was an exciting event and the finish was close between Cpl. Crane USA, and Pte. Courtenay DLI. The invitation tug-of-war caused great suspense and was finally won by the US team after a severe contest with the British. Gunner Scott of 3rd RHA walked off with the 200 metres, taking 22.7 seconds. Scott also shone in the long jump and in the relay races. The final score was America 94 points, Britain 43 points and France 25 points.

Prizes were awarded by high ranking officers of the three countries. America received a cup and a shield for winning the 1945 meeting.

Marlene Dietrich in WAAC uniform came along at the prize giving and signed autographs and displayed her million dollar legs for the benefit of the keenest photographers.

Other events reported included the opening of a new lakeside club by Junior-Commander Mary Churchill, playing of retreat by the massed pipe bands of the 52nd Lowland Division in the Kaiserdamm, the first release from HQRA for a soldier back into "civvy-street" and the opening of a Forces Study Centre in the suburb of Charlottenburg.

The first edition came out on August 3rd and the last on September 28th. It had been a lot of fun and the editors had received a number of letters most of which were published.

Mention should be made of the VJ Parade that took place in Berlin on September 7th 1945.

The war against the Japanese had come to a dramatic end when the atom bombs were dropped on Hiroshima and Nagasaki. Earlier I, with many others, had had Far East One written into my Army Paybook. We were all expecting at least another two years of war and I was dreading being sent out to the Far East to take part in some costly landing on the inhospitable shores of Japan. I was on a troop ship bound from Rotterdam to Harwich for a second leave at home when the news flash came about the atom bombing. I need hardly tell you how delighted I was to realise that Far East One would no longer mean anything in my Paybook. Whatever subsequent thoughts I have had about the morality of the atom bomb and its use in 1945, I can assure you that only joy filled my heart on August 15th.

Upon my return from leave to Berlin the big flap was preparing for the victory parade. Troops of America, Britain, France and Russia took part.

Each provided a military band, mechanised troops and infantry. It was a colourful spectacle: The saluting base and the road were lined with flags. The Soviet band was very smartly turned out in red and blue, and we saw and heard for the first time those musical bells that are so popular now with Scout and cadet bands. The British were represented by the band of the Royal Horse Guards in traditional puttees and breeches. The major interest was the arrival of the five star generals. The two most eagerly awaited were Patton (Gorgeous Georgie) and Zhukov who was resplendent behind a formidable array of medals.

The biggest spectacle were the Soviet tanks. Great monsters, these, carrying a large gun well forward, probably a 105mm, and with wide tracks reminiscent of a "Tiger". They seemed to be superior to any tank that had as yet been invented, though how mechanically sound they were was problematic.

The parade ended with the various national anthems and then jeeps fitted with police sirens cleared the crowd in order to let the Allied Generals pass.

The VJ Parade in Berlin, 7th September 1945. Above, Russian Tanks in the Parade.

Below, The saluting base, General Patton and Marshall Zhukov can be seen in the centre.

Our departure from Berlin became imminent. There was a frenzy of packing and preparation. The bombardier waiter for the officers' mess was taken ill. Someone had to be found to take charge of the mess during the move and to be responsible for the wine cellar. For some reason which I was never sure of I was approached by the mess secretary, a captain, and asked if I would take the job on until such time as the real man was able to resume duty. I said that I would. After all it would be a new experience and I might learn how the other half lived!

The night before we left a whole crowd of us went down to a bierkeller to celebrate our departure from Berlin. I had to be up and ready to lead the truck containing the mess drink at 5am. We were drinking Steinhager, a local gin from stoneware bottles. Gin and orange was a popular tipple and I liked it as well as anyone. My glass was filled and refilled a couple of times and then I insisted that I had only orange juice added. I was aware of a good deal of smiling and amusement and put it down to the generally happy atmosphere. Then my head began to swim. I got up quietly and went to the lavatory. I began to feel awful. My head swam and I thought I was going to pass out. Those rotten sods of my mates, or some of then, had been trying to get me drunk. They had been filling my glass with neat gin when I was not looking. No doubt they thought this would be a good opportunity to get at the officers. Some of them may have resented that I was to be acting mess waiter. Perhaps the driver on VE night was settling an old score when I helped to stop him going haywire in the farmhouse. Maybe again I had been seen to be too pushy with the forces newspaper.

I put my forehead against the cold concrete wall of the urinal and fought to gain a hold on myself. I would not oblige them and pass out. I would walk straight out into that evening air and walk straight back to the billet and make sure that I was awakened at 4am in order to be ready to move off at 5am.

I left the lavatory and walked out without saying a word to anyone.

At 5am next morning I mounted the passenger side of the truck and told the driver to move off and follow the vehicle in front. I felt weary but not drunk. No one ever mentioned that previous night to me, and I asked not a thing about it. It was best treated that way.

PRICE: ONE MARK

PUBLISHED BY H.Q.R.A. AND C.M.O.S.

NO. 7 BERLIN FRIDAY 14 SEPTEMBER 1945

The Berlin Bugle ran for eight weekly editions.

PRICE: ONE MARK

The Berlin Bugle

PUBLISHED BY H.Q.R.A. AND C.M.O.S.

NO. 8 BERLIN FRIDAY 21 SEPTEMBER 1945

Glamour photographs were found in a Berlin Publishers.

10

Elmshorn, Oldenburg and home

My time with the officers' mess back in Albersdorf in Holstein was short. I dispensed the drinks under the orders of the mess officer. I waited at table at evening dinner and learned not to add my own conversation to that of the diners. I generally supervised the two cooks, a charming Danish couple who had been engaged for the task. There were several German workers at the house. One was an energetic lad who had been in the navy in U-boats and told me that he had looked at New York through the periscope of the submarine that he was serving in. He had seen the Statue of Liberty, Staten island, the Hudson River crowded with shipping and the tall skyscrapers of Manhattan. He was at a loss to know what to do with himself and had attached himself to the house in order to get a bit of food. He spent most of his time chopping wood. He received no pay from the mess and was regarded as yet another hanger-on. Since the army had food many Germans hung around trying to get some kind of job. There had been one smooth talking civilian, in a well-cut suit, who had fastened himself on to HQRA in Berlin and made himself, in his own view, indispensible to the officers on account of his knowledge of the English language and the business community of the city. When he was found to have been stealing from army stores and involving himself in Black Market activities with army rations he was turfed out on to the road outside Berlin as the convoy left for Albersdorf. Protesting his innocence to the end he vanished behind us as we sped along the autobahn to the west.

After a week or two at the mess I received my marching orders. The CMOS was wound up and all personnel were posted to different units. Dennis Bould and I were to meet for the last time in a steamy canteen in the town. I was put on regimental guard duty, the first time since leaving England for the invasion. I had to smarten myself up and ensure that all the webbing was well scrubbed and the brasses clean. And what did I have to mount guard outside? Yes, none other than the HQRA house where the day before I had been the mess steward!

A week later I was delivered to J Battery of the 3rd Regiment of the Royal Horse Artillery in the town of Elmshorn. I was once more a driver/operator in a regular artillery unit equipped with 25 pounders hauled by quads. The first thing that happened was being told to unpick the crossed flags sewn onto my battledress to show that I was a signaller.

'We don't wear things like that in the RHA. You can get some brass shoulder badges from the stores that will tell the rest of the army that you are in a crack regiment'

The Royal Horse Artillery was regarded as the crack artillery mob and was in great rivalry with the 5th RHA. I soon discovered that there was a long standing antipathy between both regiments and the Brigade of Guards. The Guards Armoured Division was the butt of many jokes. The gunners used to say that they were so well-drilled that when they were spoken to in a tank they stood to attention and knocked themselves out on the turret roof! I soon fitted in with life in J Battery for it was good to be with a bunch who were real gunners and not marginal like the CMOS.

Jim Pearce and George Laidlaw came along with me so there was a nucleus of friendship. Elmshorn was a small town a few miles north of Hamburg. It was part industrial and part residential. The major industry was leather manufacture and it was here that I made friends with Rupert Masting and his wife, Irina, and their little son, Peter.

Rupert was a Latvian leather chemist who had worked in his father's plant in Riga. The factory had been taken over by the Soviets when the Red Army invaded the Baltic

Above, the author and Peter Masting.
Below, Peter with his father. Rupert Masting.

republics in 1940. Rupert had not liked the Russian occupation and the run-down of the factory (as he described it) so when the Germans took over in 1941 he got his job and his father's factory back. When the tide of war swept westward and it seemed that the Russians would yet again take over Latvia, he got the job of chemist and manager in Elmshorn. His wife was a beautiful Siberian woman, with high cheek bones and wonderful dark eyes. Their Peter was three and was beginning to speak several languages already because of his migrations. His parents did not like him playing with the German children because he picked up too many rude words and a poor accent.

At Christmas 1945 we were entertained in the Masting's flat and I have a picture somewhere of Rupert and Irina sitting by their Christmas tree. I should say that by this time the policy of non-fraternisation had been completely abandoned. Many of the soldiers stationed in Elmshorn made stable relationships with German girls. It was a popular place to be stationed in after the strains of Berlin. Rupert was very determined to come to Britain, and saw in me someone who could help him. I was willing to do what I could and asked my mother to send me some editions of a trade paper in leather manufacture. This she did and Rupert wrote after some jobs in Britain, finally securing a post in a manufactory in Clackmannanshire in Scotland.

By that time the Regiment had moved away from Elmshorn but I had the satisfaction of corresponding with the Mastings for some years after the war. I never saw them again and after about 1952 the correspondence stopped. I do not know if Rupert had died. Peter would be forty-eight years old now and if he happens to read this I would like to think he might get in touch with me through the publisher. While I was in Elmshorn I had come to the firm conclusion that I would not return to Barclays or any other bank upon my release from the army but take up teaching as a career. Little Peter played but a small part in this, for it was really my friend Maurice Tyerman, who was already a qualified teacher, that had interested me in that work and made me look at a new future. I was not to be disappointed.

One of the new experiences was learning to be a member of a tank crew. In 185 Field Regiment the OP had been a

Bren carrier to meld with the infantry vehicles. In 7th Armoured Division the artillery OP had to be a tank. I must admit to a certain childish pleasure in riding in a big "Comet" tank, the most advanced British tank at that time. The 3rd RHA was receiving new officers and men, many of whom had never fought in the war.

The CRA decided that his officers needed some practice in fire orders using live ammunition. So J Battery was despatched to Munster Lager, where there was a huge expanse of land available for military schemes, which had previously been land used by the Wehrmacht for similar purposes.

On the first day on the range the CRA invited his officers to take over control of the guns and send down some fire orders. I was the duty signaller.

'H.E.119 charge 2,' said the first officer. I repeated the order to the guns.

'Angle of sight zero.' There was a pregnant pause.

'Excuse me, sir,' I piped up, 'You have not given the bearing.'

'Oh, bearing zero 126 degrees.'

This I repeated. There was another long pause.

'Give the angle of sight again,' I hissed to the officer.

'Angle of sight zero'. he said. This I repeated to the guns.

'Fire by order.'

'Sir, you need the range.'

'Range 3,000.'

The guns received my radio message.

'Troop ready,' I passed to the officer.

'Fire' and fire was sent to the guns.

'Add four hundred.' The bracket was made and the target was centred and four rounds of gunfire were ordered.

The CRA asked another officer to take over. Nervously he looked through his binoculars at the target, an odd collection of abandoned trucks.

'Range 2,600.'

'Excuse me, sir,' I said, 'You need to give the charge first.'

'It seems to me,' said the CRA loudly, 'that only the signaller knows what he is doing.'

After the shoot was over the Battery Sergeant Major

came up to me and asked who I was and where I had come from.

To my surprise when a list of gunners to be trained for junior leadership was posted up my name was on it. Twelve of us from the three batteries were promoted to Acting Lance-Bombardier and began a course of training. I cannot for the life of me remember what we did on the course except a good deal of "square-bashing" in which we took it in turns to drill the others. This I quite enjoyed. I had enjoyed the four weeks of drilling that I had undergone in our training regiment in Burniston Barracks in Scarborough, way back in 1942. There was some satisfaction in getting the feats of drill as accurate as possible and I still like to see soldiers on parade march and handle arms in synchronisation. We felt part of a team and we felt proud to get it right. There is an element of the chorus line and of the corps de ballet in military display. I don't think I was unusual in liking drill. The other thing that I remember being involved in was a football match. I was quite hopeless at ball games and proved very little use to my team. I longed for the game to end! I was always a loner at sport, preferring to walk or run for a team although I did sometimes play hockey with better success than football and I enjoyed a game of tennis. We did have some good courts at Elmshorn and even a German professional coach. I was just beginning to improve my game when the regiment moved away.

At the end of the junior leaders course I and all the others were confirmed in the rank of Lance-Bombardier and I was paid a few more pence a week. Responsibility was not overwhelming, I was required from time to time to be the NCO in charge of the marching relief. This meant that I was the second in command of a guard detachment under a Sergeant and I had to lead the next guard out to his post, ensure he knew his duties and march the former guard back to the guard room again. It meant little sleep when on duty as I was responsible for ensuring that the guard was correctly mounted throughout the night. I also had to keep alert for the orderly officer whose job it was to come round and see that the guard was effective. You never knew at what time the orderly officer was coming. The slacker ones might not come at all. The really keen ones might turn up at 2 am on a rain-swept night!

Another duty was to act as a regimental policeman. With a sergeant or full bombardier I had to put on an armband bearing the letters "RP" and patrol the streets and enter the bars to make sure the soldiers were behaving themselves and not acting in a drunk and disorderly manner. To this end we were armed with pick handles in case we ran into trouble. Fortunately whenever I was on this task all was peaceful. I am not sure if I would have been much good in a rough house being of slight build and wearing glasses!

There was one very unpleasant task that our troop was required to do at the request of the military government. A large number of Yugoslavs, men, women and children, were occupying a displaced persons camp just out of town. It was government policy to return all displaced persons to their own country if they could be found to have one. These Yugoslavs refused to be sent back to Yugoslavia because they feared death at the hands of Marshall Tito's Communist regime. Whether this fear was well-founded or not no one knew. The military government had ordered their return and sent the army along to enforce it. And that meant us. We were fully armed with rifles and ammunition and bayonets and were formed up in a ring around the camp. The spokesman for the British Military Government parleyed with the camp leaders and then turning on his heel ordered the Yugoslavs to get into the trucks that were standing by to take them to the railhead. The campers refused to move. We were ordered to load our rifles and to take aim at the camp leaders. There were a few moments of tension, then the Yugoslav leaders moved towards the trucks followed by their wives and families. We were roundly cursed and spat at, but into the trucks they all went and they were driven away. Then the huts were demolished and the wreckage set on fire to make sure they could not be occupied again. This was all too reminiscent of the way the Germans had behaved to their subservient people and I for one was indignant about what I had seen and the part I had perforce to play in it. Many years later I can recognise the need for force to ensure that the law is obeyed, but I still wonder whether that law was not arbitrary and that the campers could not have been left where they were. Did many of them die upon their return to their homeland? We shall never know.

On a lighter note I had what might be called a solo adventure. As duty driver I was called out to take a sergeant major to Hanover airport on an emergency flight. One of his children was at the point of death and he was granted compassionate leave. Only by picking up an RAF flight could he be got home with speed. It was, I suppose some two hundred miles from Elmshorn to Hanover. We set off in my radio truck, a Chevrolet 15cwt, in the late afternoon in April 1946. It was not easy to drive at night because our maps were imperfect and the roads were still suffering from the use of war. We made the barracks in Hanover where I had been told to go and the sergeant major was hurried off in a jeep to the airport. I got some grub in the canteen and found a space on the floor somewhere and tried to sleep. Unfortunately, I had only one blanket with me and the night was cold. There was no mattress and I spent an uncomfortable night. It is strange that this experience stands out in my mind after forty-three years. I must have had many more uncomfortable nights than this one, but I can still feel the chill, feel the hard floor and in my mind touch the polished wood out of which it was made.

In the morning I had some breakfast in the canteen and having done my ablutions and rolled up the meagre blanket, I made my way to the Chev. To my dismay I spotted a flat tyre. I looked in the back of the truck for the spare and realised with a thrill of horror that I did not have one on board. That meant two things. Firstly, I would have to drive to the nearest repair unit to get the tyre fixed and secondly, I stood a very good chance of being put on a charge for driving on duty without a spare wheel. Where was the nearest repair unit? Go out on the main road towards Hildesheim and there is a big German tyre factory that will vulcanize the tyre for you, I was told by the soldiers in the barracks. So with a flat tyre I drove slowly for a mile or so until I turned into the works and tried to find a foreman. After some explanations repeated several times a couple of German mechanics took the tyre off the wheel, mended the puncture and put it back on to the wheel again. There was, of course, no question of payment. I signed some sheet for the sergeant in charge of the bay and with a happy heart drove off in the direction of Hamburg.

I had not gone more than three miles when I was aware of another flat tyre. It was the same one! So much for vaunted German workmanship! What was I to do now? I did not fancy going back to the factory. There must be a Royal Army Transport Corps unit somewhere along the road. After a mile of slow driving I pulled into a small army workshop unit at the side of the road.

'Can you help me?' I said to a couple of men working on the wheels of a giant tank transporter.

'Have a word with the corporal. He's in the hut brewing up some tea.'

The corporal heard my tale and promised that he and his men would have a look at my tyre as soon as they had finished with the tank transporter. They shared some lunch with me and then some dinner. I was lucky to have come across a bunch of good lads. It must be remembered that civilian services were almost non-existent in these early months after the end of the war, but that there were army units everywhere, many of which had relatively little to do. It should also be remembered that we were all strangers in a foreign land and willing to stick together. The wartime feeling of comradeship and mutual respect for fellow members of the armed forces was still very strong.

'Now don't you worry, lad,' said the corporal. 'We've got a spare new tyre right here and me and my mates will fit it for you. You wouldn't get far with that old tyre however well we patched it.'

I spent the night with them, once more chilly in the single blanket, but at least able to bunk down on a straw-filled mattress. In the early morning I thanked them for their help and drove away into the early morning mist. Soon I was able to turn on to the autobahn and develop a turn of speed. There was no traffic at all on the road. As I drove along as fast as I could go in the old bus I hit an unperceived hole in the road, caused by war-time shelling. The truck leapt into the air, my head hitting the roof of the cab. As the vehicle crashed down on to the road the bonnet was forced up by the bump and the engine cut out. Oh God, whatever had happened this time! Shaken, I got out of the cab and inspected the engine. All the spark plug leads had been wrenched off by the force of the landing. I switched the ignition off and carefully replaced the leads. Then, ignition on, pull the starter and away the engine should go. It did. It roared! Thank goodness there was nothing more to it! I walked round the truck looking at the wheels and the suspension. All seemed to be okay. So on I drove, stopping only to give a lift to a hitch-hiking German policeman who was standing hopefully at the road side. He wanted a lift to Hamburg and I was happy to oblige him. Had not I had a good deal of help on this round trip? One good turn deserves another, I thought.

When I reached Elmshorn an hour or so later, I drove in and parked the truck by the battery office. The transport sergeant, who had detailed me to go three days ago, hardly looked up from his paper.

'Oh, you're back are you? Did the sergeant major get his plane?' I told him that I believed he had.

'Did you have a good trip?' I said that I had had a good trip.

'Okay, then.'

Not a word about being away for three days? Nothing noticed about not having a spare wheel? I just could not believe my luck!

Later in the year the regiment moved to Oldenburg, not far from the Dutch border. We moved into what had been German army barracks on the outskirts of the sleepy old market town. The barracks were solidly built and roomy, but they were not so popular among the lads because all of the regiment were together, instead of being all around the town of Elmshorn. Every one had to pass in and out of the main gate, passing the guard room. Therefore the men were more restricted and subject to greater military discipline. It was an opportunity to get back into journalism again and I and another Mercer, named Keith but no relation of mine, joined forces with Eric Horton to bring out a fortnightly publication called *Stand Easy*.

The editorial of August 3rd 1946 has this to say:

"Without doubt the chief topic of conversation in the Regiment is Oldenburg in general, and barrack life in particular. Oldenburg is a pleasant town, and doubtless we shall all grow used to it, but Elmshorn seems a much more pleasant place in retrospect. Thoughts about Elmshorn verge upon nostalgia, for some they are heart-pangs.

The second topic is the new role of the regiment. Young soldiers, fresh from training camps of Blighty, are to descend on us in hordes. No doubt many an old sweat of A/S Group 50 will look out his battle bowler and clean up his campaign ribbons."

We had received our campaign ribbons in 7th Armoured ahead of those in other units because of our entry to Berlin. Churchill was reported to have urged that none of the early troops in Berlin were to be outdone by the Russians or Americans.

There had been a frenzy of issuing and sewing on the two ribbons, the 1939–45 Star and the France and Germany Star, just before we set off for the German capital in the previous year.

I had to await the issue of the War Medal and the medals that went with the ribbons until I was home and out of the army in 1947.

Other matters in the Regimental newspaper were a beauty contest in which the first prize winner was a Miss Dorothy Camp and the second prize winner a Miss Myra Scott. Their photographs were reproduced to prove their talent. Also a series of letters to the editor, which included one on the perennial topic of quality of tea.

"Dear Mr Editor,

The Regimental Canteen serves tea at morning break. But it is tea in name only, as usually one is charged half a mark for a cup of hot, slightly tanned water. This is even putting the railway station buffet to shame. Tea had hitherto been free and apart from occasional lapses by the Battery Cooks, it has been drinkable. Is this yet another inconvenience of barrack life?

Signed CHAR WALLAH

Finding enough copy was always a problem.

There were plenty of films for the soldiery to see. The paper gives a review of the following:

"*The Corn is Green*" with Bette Davis; "*Lady on a Train*" with Deanna Durbin; "*Brief Encounter*" with Celia Johnson and Trevor Howard; "*I know where I'm going*" with Wendy Hiller and Roger Livesey; "*Lady in the Dark*" with Ginger Rogers; "*Saratoga Trunk*" with Ingrid Bergman and Gary Cooper; "*Meet me in St Louis*" with Judy Garland.

All these could be seen in the space of a fortnight! Those were the days when the cinema was the top field of entertainment and television was still experimental.

There was a good deal of reporting of the comings and goings of personnel and in-house gossip which means little after all these years. There was also a satirical column written, I believe by one of the officers, under the psuedonym of Feste.

There was a verse in one issue that is worth reproducing. It is entitled:

WHO MADE ME A SERGEANT?

Sergeant Wenceslas looked out
On the feast of Stephen
As the Guard stood round about
Blancoed crisp and even
Loudly swore the Sarg that night
Like a London Coster
When he found a Rookie bright
Missing from the roster.

"Hither Corp and stand by me
If thou know'st it spill it
This 'ere rookie who is he
And where the hell's his billet?
"Sarg he lives a good league hence
And his name is Taffy
'Spect he's having Teas and Wads
In the nearest NAAFI,"

"Is that so? fall in two men
And we'll go and find him

And when we do, my fine old Corp
We'll on a Fizzer stick him".
Sarg and Corporal forth they went
Though the night was lousy
There they found him sweating Kard
In a game of Housy.

There he stood the next fine Morn
With two men as flankers
And got 10 days Jankers.
So beware you rookies bright
When you're warned for DUTY
Either be there on the dot or
You've had it, like this Beauty.

It was always a problem to get enough material for each fornightly edition and I expect a number of the contributions were put in by the editors.

The army made great efforts to prepare soldiers for their return to civilian life. Many courses were organised and run and soldiers were encouraged to take time out to go on them. On one of my home leaves I had been interviewed in London for entry into the Emergency Training Scheme for Teachers and had been accepted. Thus encouraged I put in for two courses and was accepted for both. The first was a geography field course held in Ghent, in Belgium. The tutor was a rather eccentric old boy. He was a captain in the Intelligence Corps, but had been a university lecturer and was soon to return to his chosen field. We looked at ox-bow lakes, studied the effects of erosion on the land and sea and visited a weather observatory near Brussels. I learned there, never to be forgotten, how difficult it is to predict the weather in North East Europe, and this problem remains still even with our satellites and electronic skills. I enjoyed the course and the application needed to make the most of it. I thought that I might teach geography one day.

The second course was more vocationally focused since it was set up for intending teachers. It was held at Gottingen, an ancient university town, famed by the statue of the Goose Girl erected in honour of the character created by the Brothers Grimm in the fairy tale. They had been professors at Gottingen and had written their stories in their spare time. The Director of the so-called College of the Rhine Army was none other than the famous archaeologist, Sir Hugh Mortimer-Wheeler, who was a Brigadier. All the students met in the Auditorium, the hall of the university, and were greeted in a humourous and scholarly speech by the Brigadier. There were many soldiers there, officers, NCO's and other ranks pursuing various courses of an academic nature. I felt that I was now beginning to get somewhere. Having left school at sixteen, this was my first taste of university life and it was short but sweet. On the intending teachers' course we had two tutors and about thirty students. Major Toswell had been a housemaster at Rugby. Captain Charlesworth had been an elementary schoolteacher. So we had it from the lips of the private sector and from the state sector of education. I thought that Toswell had the edge over Charlesworth in delivery and the ability to hold our interest: both wetted our appetites for the real thing when ever that was to be.

I made several new friends, in particular Fred Skinner and Reg Tollett, and the time spent in Gottingen was one of the happiest in my life. As well as the lectures and the set reading, we had the opportunity to visit various places of interest including the Hartz Mountains and Bad Lauterburg. One evening Fred and I noticed a poster that had been put up advertising a concert to be given in one of the colleges that very night by the distinguished pianist, Wilhelm Backhaus. We decided to go (Reg called off, it being too classical for him he said) and hastened to the hall. When we got there we found just two people, the officer responsible for organising the event and Backhaus himself. The officer apologized first to us for not having given sufficient notice and then to the elderly pianist for the abysmal attendance. He suggested that Backhaus might wish to withdraw from the intended performance but the pianist was adamant.

'I have my audience. You have been kind enough to come to hear me. I will play for you. Never mind the others.'

So Fred, the officer and I had two hours of Backhaus to ourselves. Fred was the classical enthusiast, I only the beginner (I don't know what critical position the entertainments' officer took. He may have been bored to tears with it). For my part I was initially embarrassed to sit so close to a famous musician, but then fascinated with his skill and the music that he made.

He played with all the care and technique that he would have given to an audience of two thousand. When the last notes had died away, we all thanked him and Fred and I made our get away while the officer discussed the nature of payment. Of course the pianist would be anxious to earn some money after the breakdown of all cultural activities at the end of the war, whatever the size of the audience. But I do not feel that he played just for his fee which would have been extremely modest. He played of his best because he was a true professional, living up to his own reputation. He could have done nothing less.

As the Autumn approached, the date of my release from the army drew near. I was Group 46 or 47 and expected to be home for good round about the New Year of 1947. I had been transferred into Regimental HQ to act as an assistant to the Intelligence Officer, a Captain Cadbury, who was I am almost certain a member of that famous chocolate family concern.

My job was to file papers and write up reports for Cadbury concerning the state of morale amongst the local German population. I am not sure why I had been chosen for this task. I could speak a little German and understand rather more that I could speak and I had, as an assistant editor of the Regimental journal, written some fairly bland articles on current affairs.

Anyway there I was working in the office and having a quiet time of it. Then I was approached on two sides for different tasks.

The first approach was from a major who had been in education in civilian life and had been charged with setting up a school for the children of the newly-arriving service families. I was asked to help teach in the first school in Oldenburg which would be established in a commandeered house in the town. About six children would be arriving soon with their mothers to settle into the married quarters by the barracks.

Since I intended to become a schoolteacher as soon as I could, I was delighted to accept the request. I was even more delighted when I was told that I would be made up to the rank of sergeant in order to fulfil this task.

The second approach was from the Major in command of J Battery, to which I still officially belonged. The Regiment was to go on a training scheme and as a signaller I was needed to take a part and help to train the new arrivals. I was called before him and it was clear that he did not approve of either my intelligence work or of my schoolmastering the servicemen's children.

'You are a driver/operator in my battery, Mercer,' he said, 'You got your stripe because you knew your job as a signaller. I can't allow my men to be sent off into other piffling occupations. You could become the signal sergeant of my battery if you deferred your release and signed on for another year.'

I said that I would think about staying on for another year and that I would be very willing to join in the forthcoming scheme. I was sure that Captain Cadbury would release me if the Major ordered it, and that as for the teaching, it would not be starting until well after the scheme.

Two days later the Regiment set off on its training exercise. I was the Major's signaller in a Bren carrier. The OP tank was not to be used as an economy measure as it used too much petrol. The Major was obviously annoyed about this economy which relegated the unit to the support of an infantry division. The Major was a product of a hard school of experience, having joined the army as a boy bugler and made his way up through the ranks to reach his Majority in an elite regiment. He was very proud of his remarkable achievement, but also sensitive and touchy about his importance and his responsibility. In the event the scheme was not particularly successful. For much of the time we were operating in dense pine woods with occasional wide clearings. Try as I might I kept losing radio contact which was vital to the Major's role in the exercise. When we returned to the base he turned on me in no uncertain terms.

'This is your fault the exercise has been a balls-up! You lost the radio net on purpose because you didn't want to come out into the field and give up your cushy little life in the office. I shan't forget this, Lance-Bombardier!'

I tried to protest that his accusation was not true, that it was the woods and the terrain that spoilt the radio net and that I had done my best to keep contact at all times. He ignored me and stamped away in fury. I felt extremely angry and spoke to the other Major about it. I explained that I was not the sort of person to harbour a grudge or at any time to give less than my best when working with others.

'I am sure you are telling the truth,' said the education Major. 'Don't worry about your CO. I know him pretty well and he will have forgotten all about it by the end of the week.'

This advice was probably sound but the remarks of the CO rankled me for some time and as I recall the experience now I can still summon up a feeling of resentment at being misjudged, and humiliated in front of the others.

However, I returned to the intelligence work and awaited the call to help set up the school.

Sometime in early December, the education Major sent for me and I and another soldier in the same situation as myself went to inspect the school. It was a large private house empty of all furniture.

'We have some desks and chairs on order and a couple of blackboards. All we have at the moment is a box of chalks and two orange dusters. The children are coming here next week for mornings only. If the desks have not arrived by then they'll have to sit on the floor. I hope to have some paper and some pencils. Can you get some more from your office?'

Next week came and we stood at the door of the house waiting for our first lesson. The six children had become eight. The eldest was eleven and the youngest six. Once registration had taken place I was to do some work with the younger group and my colleague with the older.

The children arrived in a truck accompanied by two of the mothers who had offered to act as general helpers and tea makers. The Major made up the register and spoke briefly to the children. They were allocated to their respective groups and I was faced with my first class of real children — all four of them! I was petrified. I had planned several activities and had pencil and paper and chalk (but no blackboard). Within ten minutes all the paper was used up, two of the pencils were broken and I was at my wits end to know what to do with them next. As the children became increasingly restless I began to try to tell them a story. This held them for a while until the spell was broken by one of them bursting out with:

'I want my mummy!'

The Major mercifully arrived on the scene and announced that it was break and tea time.

'I don't like tea,' said one of the older boys.

'No, I don't like tea either. Can we have orange juice?'

'Not today you can't. You'll have to make do with water. We'll try to get some orange cordial for you tomorrow.'

During the break two of the boys slipped away and explored upstairs. They signalled their reappearance by sliding down the bannisters. Soon all the children were climbing the stairs and sliding down the bannisters. The more enterprising climbed to the second floor and proceeded to slide down two flights of bannisters. Soon all the children were sliding down two flights of bannisters. Attempts to stop them by remonstration were of no avail. Shouting at them seemed to have no effect. The Major grabbed the first to land at the bottom and stood him against the wall of the entrance hall. As each child slid down they were duly held and moved to the wall. Soon all the children were standing quietly against the wall. The secret of controlling children as I was to learn later is to anticipate each move and make sure that you retain the initiative. What initiative the Major had up his sleeve next we never knew because at that moment of order there was a hoot from a truck outside, followed by the entrance of the driver to take them back to their homes.

'Here you are then, sir. My word, aren't the little blighters well behaved. I don't know how you manage to do it!'

Once the children were out of the building the Major roared with laughter and did not stop for over a minute.

'Well, that's a very good introduction to teaching for you,' he exclaimed to us. 'If only some of those who write books on the art of teaching could have been with us this morning. Now the first thing we must do is to fit some wooden blocks on to the bannisters so that the little perishers can't do that again!'

In fact, I never did return to that school. The Major decided to close it until the desks and other fittings and equipment had arrived, and by the time that had happened I was home and never to return. I did seriously think of staying on another year. I would have enjoyed being the signal sergeant for the Battery and would have earned some money while awaiting my entrance to teacher training college. However, I had a widowed mother back home and felt that I should return there and help to support her after nearly five years in the Army. As it turned out it was not until February 1949 that I began the college course, which was a much longer time to wait than I had expected.

I was called to the Battery Office near to Christmas and told that my promotion to sergeant had come through, backdated a month. I had to sew my stripes on immediately and report to the Sergeants' Mess. There the Regimental Sergeant Major greeted me and bought me a drink as was the custom.

'I know that you are going to be released tomorrow,' he said, 'but we must keep up the traditions. You must be the quickest promotion and release in the history of the Regiment.'

I was ill-at-ease in such lofty company. Regimental Sergeant Majors are a very special breed. They had the power to terrorise other ranks and the power to intimidate junior officers, as well. I had never been on speaking terms with a RSM before. Jumping from Lance-Bombardier to Sergeant in one go was not an easy transition to me or to the Sergeants' Mess.

I made my excuses and returned to my billet. It was not worth transferring my gear to the Mess for just one night.

In the morning I collected my "demob" papers and those of several other men who were to travel with me. It was bitterly cold weather. Snow was thick on the ground. It would be a fitting farewell to the army. General Freeze! I said farewell to my mates and we boarded a truck to take us to the station. Those waiting for the train had built a bonfire at the side of the platform mostly from the wooden

The author ready for the boat home, December 19th 1946

railings separating the station from the footpath alongside. To my amazement a number of Germans could be seen gathering wood to feed the bonfire. Why on earth should they be destroying their own property to keep the occupying troops warm? Here was the evidence for a fresh intelligence report!

The train eventually chugged in and all the men clambered aboard. The German State Railway was being run by the military government and the equipment was in a poor condition. The railways had been bombed throughout the war and the locomotives and rolling stock badly damaged. Many of the lines had been repaired but the speed of the trains was much reduced. It was common to find a speed restriction on long stretches of the track and this journey from Oldenburg to Bremerhaven was no exception.

As well as my webbing packs, I had a large wooden box which I had had specially made to contain the seventy-eight speed gramophone records that I had acquired for a song in Berlin. It was heavy and awkward, but I considered it very worthwhile to take back with me. In the slow moving train all the soldiers were huddled up in their greatcoats to keep warm for there was no heat on the train. Sleep was difficult if not well nigh impossible. In the early hours of the morning the train wheezed and puffed into Bremerhaven and came to a halt at the dockside. With painful slowness the soldiers were moved from the train to the quay and on to the ship alongside. The wind off the North Sea was a cold cutting knife. What a pleasure it was to get on to the ship and feel the heat from the ventilators blowing around you. After the freeze of the train and the quay the ship was a warm welcoming monster into whose bloodstream we willingly entered.

The crossing to Hull was relatively uneventful. It was a new ship with an American crew. The messing arrangements were new to me. Everyone lined up with a metal tray that had compartments in it. As one progressed along the galley the various items of food were plonked into separate sections. At the end of the meal, one tipped the remains into a bin and the tray was washed an returned ready for the next sitting. I suppose it was efficient and kept the foodstuffs separate, but it did not appear to me at all appetising. Moreover the food itself was not appealing in appearance or taste. In the course of the voyage the ship began to roll considerably. I believed that I was a good sailor and had experienced pitching and tossing without much trouble, but rolling was another matter. I lay on my bunk and tried not to look at anything that was swinging with the roll. The ship ploughed on through the heavy sea rolling slowly and deeply from side to side. I fought off nausea for as long as I could and then was quietly sick into the copy of *Punch* that I was trying to read.

Dawn saw a grey morning and another day at sea. I avoided food and contented myself with coffee. By the time we reached the Humber the next day the wind had dropped and I was feeling only slightly queasy. As we left the ship we were stopped by Customs.

'What do you have in that box, sergeant?' asked the customs officer. I said that it contained gramophone records that I had purchased in Berlin.

'Step this way,' and I was led into a hut accompanied by two Redcaps.

'Do you have any guns with you?' Now I began to understand why I was being viewed with suspicion. An order had been made that anyone bringing guns home as souvenirs would be liable to a long prison sentence. I had possessed some guns, but the last one, a big Italian revolver, I had dismantled and thrown piece by piece into the frozen river in Oldenburg two days before I left for the last time. The bullets I had scattered across several fields. I most certainly did not want to come back to "civvy street" and spend the remaining years of my life in gaol.

I was asked to open the box and its contents were carefully examined. My webbing was searched and all my pockets and clothing. I began to feel like a criminal.

'You'll have to pay duty on these records, sergeant. We estimate that you have to pay £15.'

Fifteen pounds! That was a small fortune in 1946! I had only paid the equivalent of £10 for them all in Berlin. Had it been worthwhile all the hassle to get them home in order to pay out so much to the excise people? So much for being a soldier for King and Country! So I paid up. I had just a few shillings left when I reached home on Christmas Eve, and was totally unexpected. It could not have happened at a more fitting time. My pleasure at being home for good was only marred by the receipt of an income tax demand for £9 on my back pay as a sergeant. It was little things like this and the customs duty that soured me to the Government. I had been proud to be a British soldier, doing an unpleasant but necessary job playing a small part in ridding the world of Nazi tyranny. But the average British serviceman was poorly treated once the war was over. The class-consciousness of the British seemed to ensure that the ordinary man was soon put back in his place, even under a Labour administration. How much more generous were the Australians, the Canadians and the Americans to their returning servicemen. There is an element of niggardliness that is perpetuated throughout our bureaucracy. And this still applies.

So I end my story on a sour note!

EPILOGUE

I kept my army greatcoat, paying the clerk at the demobilisation centre in Hull £1 for it. I was intrigued to learn that legally all greatcoats issued to the British Army came from a fund set up by Florence Nightingale as a consequence of the Crimean War and that soldiers could keep them upon discharge for this token payment. Later I had it converted by a tailor to look more like a civilian coat. Eventually after years of use I gave it away at a jumble sale.

My battledress jacket with medal ribbons and sergeant's stripes I kept in the wardrobe until 1956 when I gave it to the Hungarian Relief Fund. I don't know if anyone ever wore either of these warm articles of clothing after me. If anyone did I hope it kept them warm.

I did not join any Old Comrades Association or the Royal British Legion. I felt that they were for old-timers and not for the likes of me, the most civilian of wartime conscripts. That is until 1988 when it was drawn to my attention that I might have a story to tell and that 1989 would be the fiftieth anniversary of the outbreak of the Second World War. I discovered that there was a Normandy Veterans' Association in my area which I have joined (but not attended any meetings yet). I also found out that there was an Old Comrades Association of the 274 Battery meeting annually in Leeds. I hope to attend their dinner reunion in 1990. Dennis Bould has corresponded with me after all these years. He has informed me that Fred Dalton is still alive but Sergeant Major Jack Beckwith died some time ago. Wilf Smith did not live long after the end of the war. My brother-in-law George, to whom this book is dedicated, died in 1985. From another source I learn that Lt. Colonel Mackay-Lewis (retired as Major-General) known to us as "Charlie Handlebars" is still living aged 92.

A former schoolmaster colleague of mine, Ian Hamilton, a wartime captain in the 22nd Dragoons was in the assault on Le Havre. We discovered this mutual experience only last year. He is organising a visit to Le Havre in September 1989 and I and Maurice Tyerman hope to accompany him. It is indeed a small world!

BIBLIOGRAPHY

The Imperial War Museum

A Short History of the 7th Armoured Division: 1943–45 Anon.

A Short History of the 49th West Riding and Midland Infantry Division Hughes F.K. Stellar Press 1957

Overlord: D-Day and the Battle for Normandy 1944 Hastings M. Guild Publishing 1984